W9-BAS-230

ASPECTS OF FICTION

AND OTHER

VENTURES IN CRITICISM

BY

BRANDER MATTHEWS

NEW YORK
HARPER & BROTHERS PUBLISHERS
1896

4015

By BRANDER MATTHEWS.

TALES OF FANTASY AND FACT. Illustrated. Post 8vo, Cloth, $1 25.

HIS FATHER'S SON. A Novel of New York. Illustrated. Post 8vo, Cloth, $1 50.

THE ROYAL MARINE. An Idyl of Narragansett. Illustrated. 32mo, Cloth, $1 00.

VIGNETTES OF MANHATTAN. Illustrated. Post 8vo, Cloth, $1 50.

THIS PICTURE AND THAT. A Comedy. Illustrated. 32mo, Cloth, 50 cents.

STUDIES OF THE STAGE. With Portrait. 16mo, Cloth, $1 00.

THE DECISION OF THE COURT. A Comedy. Illustrated. 32mo, Cloth, 50 cents.

THE STORY OF A STORY, and Other Stories. Illustrated. 16mo, Cloth, $1 25.

AMERICANISMS AND BRITICISMS, with Other Essays on Other Isms. With Portrait. 16mo, Cloth, $1 00.

IN THE VESTIBULE LIMITED. A Story. Illustrated. 32mo, Cloth, 50 cents.

PUBLISHED BY HARPER & BROTHERS, NEW YORK.

PN
3335
m3
1896

Copyright, 1896, by HARPER & BROTHERS.

All rights reserved.

CONTENTS

AMERICAN LITERATURE

[This address was delivered before the National Educational Association, at Buffalo, July 8, 1896.]

AMERICAN LITERATURE

THE history of mankind is little more than the list of the civilizations that have arisen one on the ruin of the other, the Roman supplanting the Greek, as the Assyrian had been ousted by the Babylonian. The life of each of these successive civilizations was proportioned to the vitality of the ideas by which it was animated; and we cannot estimate it or even understand it except in so far as we are able to grasp these underlying principles. What the ideas were which dominated these vanished civilizations it is for us to discover for ourselves as best we may by a study of all the records they left behind them, and especially by a reverent examination of their laws, their arts, and their writings in so far as these have been preserved to us. Of all these relics of peoples now dead and gone, none is so instructive as literature, and none is so interesting; by its aid we are enabled to reconstruct the past, as we are also helped to understand the present.

Of the literatures which thus explain to us our fellow-man as he was and as he is, three seem to me pre-eminent, standing out and above the others not only by reason of the greater number of men of genius who have illustrated them, but also by reason of their own more persistent strength and their own broader variety. These three literatures are the Greek, the French, and the English.

There are great names in the other modern languages, no doubt—the names of Dante and of Cervantes and of Goethe, than which, indeed, there are none greater. In French literature, however, and in English there are not wanting names as mighty as these. Fortunately, the possession of genius is not the privilege of any one language, of any one country, or of any one century. Where French literature and English can claim superiority over Italian, Spanish, and German is rather in sustaining a higher average of excellence for a longer period of time. The literature of the Italian language, of the Spanish, and of the German has no such beadroll of writers of the first rank as illustrates the literature of the French and of the English.

There is perhaps no more manly instrument of precision than the Latin language, none which better repays the struggle for its mastery; but Latin literature, if not second-rate, when tried by the loftiest standards, is at least secondary, being transplanted from Greece and lacking resolute roots in its own soil. Nor is any dispute possible as to the high value of Hebrew literature; as Coleridge declared with characteristic insight, "sublimity is Hebrew by birth"; but Hebrew literature has not the wide range of the Greek, nor its impeccable beauty.

"Art is only form," said Georges Sand; and Goethe declared that the "highest operation of art is form-giving." If we accept these sayings there is no need to dwell on the supreme distinction of Greek literature, for it is only in Greek that we find the undying perfection of form. It is there only that we have clear and deep thought always beautifully embodied. Indeed, truth and beauty govern Greek literature so absolutely that, old as it is, it seems to us ever fresh and eternally young. After two thousand years and more it strikes us to-day as startlingly modern. Thoreau—whose own phrase was often Attic in its delicate precision —Thoreau asked, "What are the classics but the noblest recorded thoughts of man? They are the only oracles that are not decayed."

Nevertheless, the world has kept restlessly

moving since the fall of Athens, and mankind has developed needs that the Greeks knew not. As Molière puts it pithily, " The ancients are the ancients, and we are the men of to-day." There are questions in America now, and not a few of them, undreamed of in Sparta; and for the answers to these it is vain to go to Greek literature, modern as it may be in so many ways.

French literature has not a little of the moderation and of the charm of Greek literature. It is not violent; it is not boisterous, even; it is never freakish. It has balance and order and a broad sanity. It has an unfailing sense of style. It has lightness of touch, and it has also and always intellectual seriousness. The literature is like the language; and Voltaire declared that what was not clear was not French. And the language itself is the fit instrument of the people who use it and who have refined it for their needs—a people logical beyond all others, gifted in mathematics, devoid of hypocrisy, law-abiding, governed by the social instinct, inheritors of the Latin tradition and yet infused with the Celtic spirit.

To those of us who are controlled by the Anglo-Saxon ideals, whether or not we come of English stock, to those of us who adhere to

Anglo-Saxon conventions, no other literature can serve as a better corrective of our inherited tendencies than the French. The chief characteristic of English literature is energy, power often ill-restrained, vigor often superabundant. From the earliest rude war-songs of the stalwart Saxon fighters who were beginning to make the English language, to the latest short story setting forth the strife of an American mining camp, there is never any lack of force in English literature. There is always the Teutonic boldness and rudeness—the Teutonic readiness to push forward and to shoulder the rest of the world out of the way—the Teutonic independence that leads every man to fight for his own hand, like the smith in Scott's story. What we do not discover in English literature, with all its overmastering vitality, is economy of effort, the French self-control, the Greek sense of form.

French literature and English literature have existed side by side for many centuries, each of them influencing the other now and again, and yet each of them preserving its own individuality always, and ever revealing the dominant characteristics of the people speaking its language. We need not attempt to weigh them one against the other, and to measure them with a foot-rule, and to declare which is the greater. Equal they may be in the past and in the present; equal in the future they are not likely to be. The qualities which make French literature what it is tend also to keep the French race from expansion; just as the qualities which make English literature what it is have sent the English-speaking stock forth to fill up the waste places of the earth, and to wrest new lands from hostile savages or from inhospitable nature.

French was the language of the courts of Europe when English was little better than a dialect of rough islanders. When Chaucer chose his native English as the vehicle of his verse, he showed both courage and prescience —a courage and a prescience lacking in Bacon, who lived two hundred years later, and who did not feel himself insured against Time until his great work was safely entombed in Latin. Even at the beginning of the nineteenth century there were more men and women in the world speaking French than there were speaking English. But now at the end of the nineteenth century, with the steady spread of our stock into the four quarters of the world, there are more than twice as many people using English as there are using French.

And the end is not yet, for while four-fifths of those who have French for their mother-tongue abide in France or along its borders, not a third of those who have English for their mother-tongue dwell in England. Not only in England, Ireland, and Scotland is English spoken, and in all the many British colonies which encompass the globe about—it is also the native speech of the people of the United States. English is the language of the stock which bids fair to prove itself the most masterful, hardy, and prolific, and which seems to possess a marvellous faculty for assimilating members of other allied stems and of getting these newly received elements to accept its own hereditary ideals.

English literature is likely, therefore, to become in the future relatively more important and absolutely more influential. As there has been no relaxing of energy among the peoples that now speak the English language, probably there will be no alteration of the chief characteristic of English literature, although in time the changes of environment must make more or less modification inevitable. It will be curious to see in a century how the ideals and the practices of the race will alter, after the race is no longer pent up in an island, after it

has scattered itself over the world and assimilated other elements and adjusted itself to
other social organizations.   Here in America
we can see already some of these results, for
already is the American differentiated from
the Englishman.   We may not be able to
declare clearly wherein the difference consists;
but we all recognize it plainly enough.

Colonel Higginson has suggested that the
American has an added drop more of nervous
fluid than the Englishman.   It is perhaps apparent already that the American is swifter
than the Englishman, slighter in build, spring-
ier in gait.   Social changes are as evident as
physical.   Lowell remarked that if it was a
good thing for an English duke that he had no
social superior, it surely was not a bad thing
for a Yankee farmer.   Socially the American
is less girt in by caste than the Englishman.
These differences, obvious in life, are visible also
in literature.   We feel now, even if we do not
care to define, the unlikeness of the writing of
the British authors to the writing of the American authors.   Neither man nor nature is the
same in Great Britain as it is in the United
States; and of necessity, therefore, there cannot
be any identity between the points of view of
the men of letters of the two countries.

In time, as there come to be more writers in Canada, we shall have a perspective from yet another point of view; and in due season others will be presented to us from Australia and from India. No doubt these future authors will cherish the tradition of English literature as loyally as we Americans cherish it here in the United States — as loyally as the British cherish it in the little group of islands which was once the home of the ancestors of us all. Race characteristics are inexorable, and it is very unlikely that there will ever be any irreconcilable divergence between these separate divisions of the English-speaking peoples. English literature will continue to flourish as sturdily as ever after the parent stem has parted into five branches. All of these branches will take the same pride in their descent from a common stock and in their possession of a common literature and of a common language. A common language, I say, for the English language belongs to all those who use it, whether they live in London or in Chicago or in Melbourne.

It is not a little strange that it should now ever be needful to say that the British have no more ownership of the English language than we Americans have. The English language is

the mother-tongue of the inhabitants of the
British Isles, but so is it also the mother-tongue
of the inhabitants of the United States.   It is
not a loan to us, which may be recalled; it is
not a gift, which we have accepted; it is a
heritage, which we derived from our fore-
fathers.   We hold it by right of birth, and our
title to it is just as good as the title of our kin
across the sea.   No younger brother's portion
is it that we claim in the English language, but
a whole and undivided half. It is an American
possession as it is a British possession, no more
and no less; and we hold it on the same terms
that our cousins do.   We have the rights of
ownership, and the responsibilities also, exactly
as they have and to exactly the same extent.
The English language belongs to us also; it is
ours to use as we please, just as the common
law is ours, to modify according to our own
needs; it is ours for us to keep pure and
healthy; and it is ours for us to hand down to
our children unimpaired in strength and in
subtlety.

And as the language is a possession common
to all the English-speaking peoples, so also is
the literature.   A share in the fame of Chaucer
and of Shakespeare, of Milton and of Dryden,
is part of the inheritance of every one of us

who has English for his mother-tongue, whatever his father-land. If there be anywhere a great poet or novelist or historian, it matters not where his birth or his residence or what his nationality, if he makes use of the English language he is contributing to English literature. To distinguish the younger divisions of English literature from the elder, we shall have to call that elder division British; meaning thereby that portion of our common literature which is now produced by those who were left behind in the old home when the rest of the family went forth one by one to make their way in the world. Thus English literature, which was one and undivided till the end of the eighteenth century, has now in the nineteenth century two chief divisions—British and American; and it bids fair in the twentieth century to have three more—Canadian, Australian, and Indian.

Some such distinction between the several existing divisions of the English literature of our own time is needful, and it will be found useful. Absurd and very misleading is the antithesis sometimes made between American literature and English, since the American is but one of the divisions of the English literature of our time. Not long ago a pupil of one of the best private schools in New York maintained that American literature is just as important as English literature, producing in proof two companion manuals, of the same size externally, although of course internally on a wholly different scale. Such a lack of proportion in the treatment of different parts of the literature of the English language is foolish and harmful. But a comparison of American literature with the merely British literature of to-day might be proper enough. What we need to grasp clearly is the fact that the stream of English literature had only one channel until the end of the last century, and that in this century it has two channels. The new mouth that this massive current has made for itself is American;—and so we are compelled to call the old mouth British.

Through which of these channels the fuller stream shall flow in the next century no man can foretell to-day. It is a fact that the population of these United States is now nearly twice as large as the population of the British Isles, and not inferior in ability or in energy. But it is a fact also that in America a smaller proportion of the ability and the energy of the people seems to be devoted to the cause of letters. In a new country life itself offers the widest opportunities; and literature here has keener rivals and more of them than it can have in a land which has been cleared and tilled and tended since a time whereof the memory of man runneth not to the contrary. The earliest Americans had other duties than the writing of books: they had to lay deep the broad foundations of this mighty nation. It was more than two hundred years after the establishment of the first trading-post on the island of Manhattan when Washington Irving published the 'Sketch Book,' the first work of American authorship to win a wide popularity beyond the borders of our own country —before Fenimore Cooper a little later published the 'Spy,' the first work of American authorship to win a wide popularity beyond the borders of our own language. We may say that American literature is now but little older than the threescore years and ten allotted as the span of a man's natural life.

We had had authors, it is true, in the eighteenth century, and at least two of these, Jonathan Edwards and Benjamin Franklin, hold high rank; but it was not until towards the end of the first quarter of the nineteenth century that we began really to have a literature. It is scarcely an overstatement to say that there are men alive to-day who are as old as American literature is. But in the past three-quarters of a century American literature has taken root firmly and blossomed forth abundantly and spread itself abroad sturdily. Emerson followed Edwards and Franklin. Hawthorne and Poe came after Irving and Cooper. Bryant proved that Nature here in America was fit for the purposes of Art; and he was succeeded by Longfellow and Lowell, by Whittier and Holmes.

During these same threescore years and ten there were great writers in the other branch of the literature of our language, in British literature, perhaps greater writers than there were here in America, and of a certainty there were more of them. There is no need now to call the roll of the mighty men of letters alive in England at the middle of this century. But much as we admire these British authors, much as we respect them, I do not think that they are as close to us as the authors of our own country; we do not cherish them with the same affection. Just as the modern literatures are nearer to us than the ancient, because we ourselves are modern, just as English literature is nearer to us than French, because we ourselves speak English, so the

American division of that literature is closer to us than the British. It helps us to understand one another, and it explains us to ourselves. If we accept the statement that, after all, literature is only a criticism of life, it is of value in proportion as its criticism of life is truthful. Surely it needs no argument to show that the life it is most needful for us Americans to have criticised truthfully is our own life. It is only in our own literature that we can hope to learn the truth about ourselves; and this indeed is what we must always insist upon in our literature—the truth, the whole truth, and nothing but the truth. Lowell reminded us that Goethe went to the root of the matter when he said that "people are always talking of the study of the ancients; yet what does this mean but apply yourself to the actual world and seek to express it, since this is what the ancients did when they were alive?"

As we consider the brief history of the American branch of English literature, we can see that the growth of a healthy feeling in regard to it has been hindered by two unfortunate failings—provincialism and colonialism. By provincialism I mean the spirit of Little Pedlington, the spirit that makes swans of all

2

our geese. By colonialism I mean the attitude of looking humbly towards the old country for guidance and for counsel even about our own affairs.

Provincialism is local pride unduly inflated. It is the temper that is ready to hail as a Swan of Avon any local gosling who has taught himself to make an unnatural use of his own quills. It is always tempting us to stand on tiptoe to proclaim our own superiority. It prevents our seeing ourselves in proper proportion to the rest of the world. It leads to the preparation of school-manuals in which the three-score years and ten of American literature are made equal in importance to the thousand years of literature produced in Great Britain. It tends to render a modest writer, like Longfellow, ridiculous by comparing him implicitly with the half-dozen world-poets. In the final resort, no doubt, every people must be the judge of its own authors; but before that final judgment is rendered every people consults the precedents and measures its own local favorites by the cosmopolitan and eternal standards.

Colonialism is shown in the timid deference towards foreign opinion about our own deeds and in the unquestioning acceptance of the foreign estimate upon our own writers. It might be defined almost as a willingness to be second-hand, a feeling which finds satisfaction in calling Irving the American Goldsmith; Cooper, the American Scott; Bryant, the American Wordsworth; and Whittier, the American Burns. Fifty years ago, when this silly trick was far more prevalent than it is now, Lowell satirized it in the 'Fable for Critics':

Why, there's scarcely a huddle of log-huts and shan-
ties
That has not brought forth its Miltons and Dantes;
I myself know ten Byrons, one Coleridge, three Shel-
leys,
Two Raphaels, six Titians (I think), one Apelles,
Leonardos and Rubenses plenty as lichens;
One (but that one is plenty) American Dickens,
A whole flock of Lambs, any number of Tennysons,
In short, if a man has the luck to have any sons
He may feel pretty certain that one out of twain
Will be some very great person over again.

And elsewhere in the same poem Lowell protests against the literature that

suits each whisper and motion
To what will be thought of it over the ocean.

The corrective of colonialism is a manly self-respect, a wholesome self-reliance, a wish

to stand firmly on our own feet, a resolve to
survey life with our own eyes and not through
any imported spectacles.   The new world has
already brought forth men of action—Washington, for example, and Lincoln—worthy of comparison with the best that the old world has
enrolled on her records.   Has the new world
produced any man of letters of corresponding
rank? Matthew Arnold thought that there
were only five world-classics—Homer, Dante,
Shakespeare, Milton, and Goethe.   This seems
a list unduly scanted; but it would need to be
five times larger before it included a single
American name.   What of it? Even if the
American poets are no one of them to be in-
scribed among the twoscore chief singers of
the world, they are not the less interesting to
us Americans, not the less inspiring.   When
an English author suggested to Sainte - Beuve
that he did not think Lamartine an important
poet, the great French critic suavely answered,
" He is important to us !" Without Lamartine there would be a blank in French literature.   So we Americans may see clearly the defects of Bryant and of Whittier, and yet we may
say that they are important to us, even though
they, like Lamartine, are not among the foremost poets of their language or of their century.

Colonialism and provincialism, although they seem mutually destructive, still manage somehow to exist side by side in our criticism to-day. The best cure for them is a study of the two other great literatures, Greek and French. Too much attention to contemporary British literature is dangerous for us, since its chief characteristics are ours by inheritance. Matthew Arnold held that it was a work of supererogation for Carlyle to preach earnestness to the English, who already abounded in that sense. For us to follow the lead of the British in literature or in any other art is but saying ditto to ourselves. It is like the marriage of cousins—and for the same reasons to be deplored. But the study of Greek literature supplies us instantly with the eternal standards, the use of which cannot but be fatal to provincialism. And the study of French literature, which is as modern as our own and yet as different as may be in its ideals and its methods, is likely to serve as a certain antidote to colonialism.

The study of Greek literature, the greatest of the literatures of the past, and the study of French literature, the other great literature of the present, will lead us towards that American cosmopolitanism which is the antithesis of both provincialism and colonialism. An American

cosmopolitanism, I say, for I agree with Coleridge in thinking that "the cosmopolitanism
which does not spring out of, and blossom
upon, the deep-rooted stem of nationality or
patriotism, is a spurious and rotten growth."
"Stendhal," a Frenchman who did not care for
France and who found himself, at last, a man
without a country, had for a motto, "I come
from Cosmopolis." A fit motto for an American author might be "I go to Cosmopolis"—
I go to see the best the world has to offer, the
best being none too good for American use;
I go as a visitor, and I return always a loyal
citizen of my own country.

As Plutarch tells us, "it is well to go for a
light to another man's fire, but not to tarry by
it, instead of kindling a torch of one's own."
A torch of one's own!—that is a possession
worth having, whether it be a flaming beacon
on the hill-top or a tiny taper in the window.
We cannot tell how far a little candle throws
its beams, nor who is laying his course by its
flickering light. The most that we can do—
and it is also the least that we should do—is
to tend the flame carefully and to keep it
steady.

(1896.)

TWO STUDIES OF THE SOUTH

TWO STUDIES OF THE SOUTH

"ONLY the literature of a country teaches us to understand its institutions," said one of the acutest of modern French critics, the late J. J. Weiss, in a recent volume of essays; and he added, with perhaps not quite the same proportion of truth, that "to the historian, who grows pale over them, collections of ordinances, codes, and constitutions yield only lifeless laws." That the laws afford us only the skeleton of a dead and gone society we may admit; and we are quick to see that it is literature which cases these bare bones in flesh and blood. Unless its literature is rooted in truth, a civilization may pass away and be misjudged —honestly misjudged, in good faith misunderstood—even at the moment of its passing. Such, so Mr. Thomas Nelson Page declares, has been the fate of the Old South; it has had no historian, and so it is in danger of perpetual misinterpretation; its civilization left no literature; and of its laws the best known is

the slave code. The one book which deals
with the life of the Old South, and which has
gone to the farthest corners of the earth, is
the one book by which the lovers of the Old
South do not wish to see it judged—'Uncle
Tom's Cabin.' The one book which was
actually written in the South between 1825
and 1850, and which seems to me to give the
most accurate account of one aspect of Southern civilization, is Mrs. Kemble's 'Journal of
a Residence on a Georgia Plantation'; and
that again is not a book by which the lovers of the Old South would wish to see it
judged.

Why was it that the Old South contributed
so little to the literature of America? Why
was it that before the war Mrs. E. D. E. N.
Southworth flourished and Mrs. Caroline Lee
Hentz? Why is it that immediately after the
war we had only the encyclopædic romances
of Mrs. Augusta J. Evans and the saccharine
stories of 'Christian Reid,' as remote from
reality as though they had been translated
from the French of Georges Ohnet or from
the German of "E. Marlitt"? Why was it that
Brer Rabbit, having had his misadventure with
the Tar Baby in countless plantations throughout the South before the war, found no Uncle

Remus to come forward and tell them for our delight until long after the war?

These are questions which every student of American literary history must put to himself sooner or later; and there are many other questions like these. For an answer one cannot do better than turn to two books which were published early in the last decade of the nineteenth century—two studies of the South, by two representative Southern writers. One of these books is the biography of 'William Gilmore Simms,' prepared for the American Men of Letters Series by Professor William P. Trent; and the other is Mr. Thomas Nelson Page's volume of essays on the 'Old South.' Both books are welcome; both are candid and honest; both are unusually well written, Professor Trent's having the solid framework of the historian, and Mr. Page's having the warm coloring of the poet. Both books, moreover, are the product of that young, hearty, loyal, and energetic New South, which is the best legacy the Old South left to the Union. Mr. Page, as becomes a poet, has a fondness for the past, while Professor Trent, as is fit in one who is instructing youth, has his face set resolutely towards the future.

There are yet a few Southern writers who

turn their backs on the present and prefer to abide amid moribund memories. Professor Trent is not one of these. He is willing to let the dead past bury its dead. In this volume we find a new spirit—a spirit not frequent even now in works of Southern authorship. His book is solid in research, worthy in workmanship, dignified in manner, and brave in tone ; it is not only a good book, it is a good deed. It is emphatically a proof of the existence of that New South which has been so loudly proclaimed and so often. In telling the career of William Gilmore Simms, Professor Trent has taken occasion to sketch for us also the environment which made Simms what he was— which, indeed, kept him from being more than he was. Believing " that Simms was a typical Southerner," Professor Trent thinks that it would be " impossible to convey a full idea of his character without a constant reference to the history of the Southern people during the first seven decades of this century." As this history has been little studied and still less understood, Professor Trent has been led to present it with a fulness of treatment which at first may seem disproportionate, but which at least has resulted in giving to his book a breadth and an interest not possible, if it had been merely the biography of William Gilmore Simms. The life of the author of 'Guy Rivers' and of the 'Yemassee' is here set down thoroughly and once for all; but accompanying it is a study of the literary conditions of the South, such as no one has ever before attempted.

Only one of Mr. Page's papers is devoted specifically to the literature of the South, but scattered throughout his book are passages which cast a sudden and a penetrating light on the social conditions of the South before the war, and thus explain the circumstances and the conditions under which that literature was produced. Here, for example, is one passage: "The social life formed of these elements in combination was one of singular sweetness and freedom from vice. . . . They were a careless and pleasure - loving people; but, as in most rural communities, their festivities were free from dissipation. There was sometimes too great an indulgence on the part of young men in the State drink, the julep; but whether it was that it killed early, or that it was usually abandoned as the responsibilities of life increased, an elderly man of dissipated habits was almost unknown. . . . The life was gay. In addition to the perpetual round of ordinary entertainment, there was always on hand or in prospect some more formal festivity—a club meeting, a fox-hunt, a party, a tournament, a wedding. Little excuse was needed to bring them together where every one was social, and where the great honor was to be the host. Scientific horse-racing was confined to the regular race-tracks, where the races were not little dashes, but four-mile heats, which tested speed and bottom alike. But good blood was common, and a ride even with a girl in an afternoon generally meant a dash along the level through the woods, where, truth to tell, she was very apt to win. Occasionally there was even a dash from the church. . . . The chief sport, however, was fox-hunting. It was, in season, almost universal. Who that lived in Old Virginia does not remember the fox-hunts—the eager chase after 'grays' or 'old reds?'"

This is a beautiful picture of a lovely life; but such an existence was too luxurious, too easy-going, too enervating for the cultivation of letters. Literature is not an affair of slippers and arm-chair, of mint-julep and fox-hunt; it is a task, a toil, unceasing and unresting; it is a labor of love, no doubt, but none the less a labor. Literature is like the other arts, a jealous mistress, and she refuses her favors to all who do not woo her with single-hearted devotion. This devotion literature received from no Southerner in the old days except from Poe. Literature did not receive this devotion from Simms, as Professor Trent makes clear to us; and Simms was a man of ability who, under more favorable conditions and under a stimulus to sterner self-discipline, might have left a book likely to last.

Of ability there was never any lack in the South. As Mr. Page says: "The causes of the absence of a Southern literature are to be looked for elsewhere than in intellectual indigence. The intellectual conditions were such as might well have created a noble literature, but the physical conditions were adverse to its production and were too potent to be overcome."

And he declares that the following were the principal causes which deprived the South of literature:

1. The people of the South were an agricultural people, widely diffused, and lacking the stimulus of immediate mental contact.

2. The absence of cities, which in the history of literary life have proved literary foci

essential for its production, and the want of publishing houses at the South.

3. The exactions of the institution of slavery, and the absorption of the intellectual forces of the people of the South in the solution of the vital problems it engendered.

4. The general ambition of the Southern people for political distinction, and the application of their literary powers to polemical controversy.

5. The absence of a reading public at the South for American authors, due in part to the conservatism of the Southern people.

That all five of these causes were potent there is no doubt. But I wonder how it is that Mr. Page did not note that four of these five causes are as potent now as they were before the war. Slavery has disappeared, that is the only change; the other conditions are much the same. And yet that the New South has a literature to-day she does not need to declare, for whoever reads our language knows the books of the new writers who have sprung up since slavery was abolished. Mark Twain has written about life on the Mississippi and Mr. Cable about the creoles of New Orleans; Mr. Harris has given us Georgia sketches in black and white, and Mr. Page himself has

painted the young men and maidens of Old
Virginia; Charles Egbert Craddock has taken
us up into the mountains of Tennessee; and
half a score of other authors have revealed to
us nooks of the earth and types of humanity
hitherto unsuspected. Yet the people of the
South are still agricultural, still ambitious of political distinction, still without cities and without publishing houses and without a wide reading public — for these new Southern authors
have been brought out at the North, in Northern magazines, and by Northern publishers.

This leads us to believe that of the five
causes given by Mr. Page one was more important than all the rest. This one was slavery.
There was, I think, another cause not given by
Mr. Page, but to this I shall return later. That
slavery was at bottom really responsible for
the Southern abstention from literature is evident to any impartial reader of Mr. Page's
volume and of Professor Trent's. As Mr. Page
himself puts it, " the standard of literary work
[in the South before the war] was not a purely
literary standard, but one based on public
opinion, which in its turn was founded on the
general consensus that the existing institution
was not to be impugned, directly or indirectly,
on any ground or by any means whatsoever.

3

This was an atmosphere in which literature could not flourish. In consequence, where literature was indulged in, it was in a half - apologetic way, as if it were not altogether compatible with the social dignity of the author. Thought which in its expression has any other standard than fidelity to truth, whatever secondary value it may have, cannot possess much value as literature." And Professor Trent again and again makes the same declaration, telling us that "a Southerner had to think in certain grooves."

Professor Trent also makes clear to us the little-understood fact that the Southerners "retained a large element of the feudal notion." So we see that "slavery helped feudalism, and feudalism helped slavery." "If feudal England was merry England," says Professor Trent in a passage I cannot forbear to quote, "the feudal South was the merry and sunny South; nay, more, it was 'a nation of men of honor and of cavaliers.' The South was never barbarous, for it possessed a picturesque civilization marked by charm of mind and manners both in men and women. But the South had forgotten that, in the words of Burke, 'the age of chivalry is gone.' It ignored the fact that while chivalry was a good thing in its day, modern civilization is a much higher thing. Even now many otherwise well informed gentlemen do not understand the full meaning of the expression 'Southern chivalry,' which they use so often. They know that it stands for many bright and high things, but they seem to forget its darker meaning. They forget that it means that the people of the South were leading a primitive life — a life behind the age. They forget that it means that Southerners were conservative, slow to change, contented with the social distinctions already existing. They forget all this, but the expression has meanings which probably were never known to them. It means that Southerners lived a life which, though simple and picturesque, was nevertheless calculated to repress many of the best faculties and powers of our nature. It was a life affording few opportunities to talents that did not lie in certain beaten grooves. It was a life gaining its intellectual nourishment, just as it did its material comforts, largely from abroad—a life that choked all thought and investigation that did not tend to conserve existing institutions and opinions— a life that rendered originality scarcely possible except under the guise of eccentricity."

In considering the Southern attitude towards

slavery, both Mr. Page and Professor Trent
point out the fact that the Southern feeling
against slavery was growing at the time of
the Revolution. That it suddenly changed
was due probably as much to the invention
of the cotton-gin as to anything else. If
that Connecticut Yankee, Eli Whitney, had
not whittled out his machine, slavery would
perhaps have disappeared as peaceably from
Virginia and North Carolina and Georgia as it
had done from New York and New Jersey and
Pennsylvania. But Eli Whitney did invent
the gin which made cotton king, and the necessity for slave labor became at once apparent.
And at this juncture, when slavery was sharply
changed from a disappearing evil to a sacred
institution, feudalism was also resuscitated by
the vogue of the Waverley novels.

There is in Mark Twain's book on the Mississippi a strong statement of the evil wrought
in the South by Sir Walter Scott's stories.
After remarking that the French revolution
and its product, Napoleon, did much harm—
but they did also this good, they broke up the
feudal system, root and branch—he arraigns
the author of 'Ivanhoe' in this wise: "Then
comes Sir Walter Scott with his enchantments,
and by his single might checks this wave of

progress and even turns it back; sets the world in love with dreams and phantoms; with decayed and swinish forms of religion; with decayed and degraded systems of government; with the sillinesses and emptinesses, sham grandeurs, sham gauds, and sham chivalries of a brainless and worthless long-vanished society. He did measureless harm—more real and lasting harm, perhaps, than any other individual that ever wrote. Most of the world has now outlived good part of these harms, though by no means all of them; but in our South they flourish pretty forcefully still. Not so forcefully as half a generation ago, perhaps, but still forcefully. There, the genuine and wholesome civilization of the nineteenth century is curiously confused and commingled with the Walter Scott middle-age sham civilization, and so you have practical common sense, progressive ideas and progressive works mixed up with the duel, the inflated speech, and the jejune romanticism of an absurd past that is dead, and out of charity ought to be buried. . . . Enough is laid on slavery, without fathering upon it these creations and contributions of Sir Walter."

Slavery and feudalism, either of them, would make literature difficult; both of them together

made it impossible. And lack of independence
of thought combined with the fascination of
the pseudo-chivalric to encourage the acceptance of foreign standards in literature; to keep
the Southern people, in fact, in an attitude of
colonial dependence to Great Britain at the
very time that the North was developing
authors of its own. Cooper to-day keeps his
place close at the heels of Scott, while Simms
is fading into oblivion as fast as G. P. R. James,
with whose work his may fairly be compared,
although Simms was probably far richer in
native gifts.

Now slavery is dead and feudalism has
departed, and with them is disappearing the
pseudo-chivalry which made the books of the
Southland ridiculous. Though oratory still
survives in the South, and though he who
"orates" is often tempted into perfervid
rhetoric, there are now not wanting writers
who take their stand on the solid realities of
life. The new authors of the New South are
not now making second-hand imitations of
foreign romance. They have come to the
knowledge of the great discovery that literature consists not so much in the mere making
up of stories as in the frank telling of the truth.
With the abolition of slavery came the freedom

to speak the truth, with an eye single to nature, without any squint around the corner to be sure that the truth might not perhaps interfere somewhere with the peculiar institution. With the departure of feudal ideals came the ability to see that life as it is—the every-day existence of the plain people—is the stuff of which literature is made. Nowadays any one who chooses to read any American magazine can assure himself that the writers of the South have laid firm hold of the "principle of literary art," to quote Professor Trent, " which requires that a man should write spontaneously and simply about those things he is fullest of and best understands."

(1892.)

THE PENALTY OF HUMOR

THE PENALTY OF HUMOR

WHEN the time came for the people of the thirteen united colonies to proclaim to the world that they were free, and that they held themselves absolved from all allegiance to the British crown, and that all political connection between them and Great Britain was totally dissolved, a committee of the Continental Congress was appointed to draw up a declaration of independence. The members of this committee were Benjamin Franklin, of Pennsylvania; John Adams, of Massachusetts; Roger Sherman, of Connecticut; Robert R. Livingston, of New York, and Thomas Jefferson, of Virginia. Why was it that their colleagues committed the writing of the Declaration of Independence to Thomas Jefferson, and not to Benjamin Franklin? The Virginian was not the most prominent man even of his own section, and although his reputation could not fairly be termed local, it was but little more, while the name of the Pennsylvanian was well

known throughout the whole civilized world.
Franklin was not only the foremost citizen of
Philadelphia, where the Congress was sitting,
he was the most experienced publicist and the
most accomplished man of letters in all the
thirteen colonies ; and he was especially well
equipped for the drawing up of an appeal to
Europe, as he had but just returned from London, where he had been pleading the cause of
his countrymen with indomitable courage and
indisputable skill. Yet Franklin was not asked
to write the Declaration of Independence ; and
although he and Adams made a few verbal
amendments, the credit of that great state
paper belongs to Jefferson. And why was it
that this responsibility was placed on Jefferson and not on Franklin?

I think the explanation lies in the fact that
Franklin was a humorist. Not only was Franklin's sturdy common-sense felt to be too plain
a homespun for wear in the courts of Europe
when the thought needed to be attired in all
the lofty rhetoric that the most fervid enthu-
siasm could produce, but also, I fear me greatly, his colleagues were afraid that Franklin
would have his joke. It would be a good
joke, no doubt—probably a very good joke ;
but the very best of jokes would not be in

keeping with the stately occasion. They were acute, those leaders of the Continental Congress, and they knew that every man has the defects of his qualities, and that a humorist is likely to be lacking in reverence, and that the writer of the Declaration of Independence had a theme which demanded the most reverential treatment.

So it was that Benjamin Franklin had to pay the penalty of humor in the last century, just as Abraham Lincoln had to pay it in this century. Because Lincoln was swift to seize upon an incongruity, and because he sought relief for his abiding melancholy in playfulness, there were not a few who refused to take him seriously. Even after his death there were honest folk who held the shrewdest and loftiest of our statesmen to have been little better than a buffoon. Of the three greatest Americans, Franklin, Washington, and Lincoln, two were humorists; and it is perhaps his deficiency of humor which makes Washington seem more remote from us and less friendly than either of the others.

" Never dare to be as funny as you can," is probably a good motto for all men in public life. No doubt the British statesman who was born in the same year as Lincoln has found his deficiency in humor an absolute advantage to him; and no doubt a potent factor of Mr. Gladstone's success has been his inability to discover anything absurd in the solemn refutation of a novel like 'Robert Elsmere' by the Prime-Minister who rules the mighty British Empire. Of course it was not merely because they were wits that Canning and Beaconsfield were distrusted; but beyond all question their ability to barb an epigram made it harder for them to keep their hold on their party. If they had been as impervious to a joke as Mr. Gladstone is, Canning and Disraeli would have found it much easier to wring from the British public due appreciation of their political sagacity. Like all other luxuries, the perpetration of an epigram has to be paid for.

Ample as the English vocabulary is to-day, since it has been enriched with the spoils of every other speech, and opulent as it is in semi-synonyms for the expression of delicate shades of difference in meaning, it is sometimes strangely deficient in needful terms, and often we find ourselves sorely at a loss for a word to indicate a necessary distinction. Thus it is that we have nothing but the inadequate phrase *sense of humor* to denominate a quality which is often carelessly confounded with *hu-*

mor itself, and which should always be sharply discriminated from it. Humor is positive, while the sense-of-humor is negative. A man with humor may make a joke, and a man with the sense-of-humor may take one. Neither includes the other; for a man able to make a joke may be incapable of taking one. From an inadequate sense-of-humor many a humorist is guilty of taking himself too seriously.

Carlyle, for instance, had humor, and not the sense-of-humor. Mr. John Morley has called Carlyle a "great transcendental humorist," and a great humorist Carlyle was, even if he were great in no other way; but Carlyle was so devoid of the sense-of-humor that he seems never to have suspected how comic a spectacle he presented vehemently preaching the virtue of silence in not less than forty successive volumes. Dickens also was a humorist and nothing else; but Dickens took himself so seriously that he broke with *Punch* because that journal refused to publish his account of his quarrel with the wife he had promised to love, cherish, and protect. Probably, also, if the sense-of-humor had been more acutely developed in Dickens he would have spared us the blank-verse pathos of his dying children; he might even have refrained from out-heroding Herod in his massacre of the innocents.

These two qualities, humor and the sense-of-humor, seem to me to be wholly distinct, and it is really a misfortune that the terms for differentiating them are so unsatisfactory. If we had sharply contrasting words for the positive humor, which is creative, and for the negative humor, which is mainly critical, we should not be forced to the paradoxical declaration that humorists have often no sense-of-humor. A friend of mine now makes it a rule never to risk a gibe with funny men, because he had twice ventured to crack a joke with accredited wits, and they both failed to take it, turning the merry jest into a serious matter. Of the two qualities, therefore, the sense-of-humor is the more highly to be prized. It is an invaluable possession, adding an unfailing savor to the enjoyment of life; and any woman who may chance to be endowed with it is always company for herself. It is so good a thing that one can hardly have too much of it, although an ardent reformer might find that an excess of it chilled the heat of his resolution.

As it is an advantage of the sense-of-humor that it prevents you from taking yourself too seriously, so it is a disadvantage of humor itself that it prevents others from taking you seriously. And there is the danger, also, that those who possess humor are sometimes possessed by it. They may thus be led to the perpetration of incongruities they would be the swiftest to perceive in another. Lowell was a poet and a humorist; but the poet wrote the lofty poem the 'Cathedral'; the humorist was responsible for the jarring note when one of the two Englishmen met beneath the shadow of the church at Chartres took the American for a Frenchman:

'Esker vous ate a nabitang?' he asked.
'I never ate one; are they good?' asked I.

In the 'Biglow Papers' the poet and the humorist were one being, not two separate entities, and the result of the fusion is the finest satire in our language since the 'Hudibras' of the Butler whose wit Lowell abundantly appreciated. But even the author of the 'Biglow Papers' had to pay the penalty of humor. Because the Yankee dialect of Hosea was phonetically represented with artistic feeling and scientific precision, the British pirates lying in wait for books of "American humor" published the 'Biglow Papers' as though it was a fit com-

panion for the misspelt writings of Artemus
Ward. It is a fact that before he was appointed minister of the United States at the
Court of St. James, Lowell was known to the
British not as the poet, the scholar, the critic,
but rather as the rival of Josh Billings. If he
had not been a humorist, Lowell might have
been wholly unknown to the readers of Great
Britain; and perhaps this would have been
better than to be greeted as an emulator of
those purveyors of "comic copy" who kept a
misfit orthography as the leading article of
their stock in trade.

And yet why should we think the less of a
poet for that he has made us laugh? As Lowell himself has said: "Let us not be ashamed
to confess that, if we find the tragedy a bore,
we take the profoundest satisfaction in the
farce. It is a mark of sanity." But if this
confession were the only mark of sanity, how
few of us could get a clean bill of health! We
are ashamed of our laughter; often we think
it a thing to be apologized for. Nor do we
thank the author of the farce for the profound
satisfaction we take in it; and appreciation of
the broad fun of farce is more often than not
semi-contemptuous, as though it were an easy
matter to make people laugh. It is, indeed,

as easy to make them laugh as to make them weep, and no easier. Heine protested against our praising the tragic poet for his faculty of drawing tears—" a talent which he has in common with the meanest onion."

In the theatre farce is looked down on even by those who prefer it. Yet farce is a legitimate form of the drama of the most honorable antiquity. It is a form of the drama in which Aristophanes and Plautus delighted, in which Shakespeare and Molière wrote masterpieces, in which Goldsmith and Sheridan excelled, in which Regnard and Labiche revelled. It is a form of the drama having not only the high authority of these great names, but having also at all times enjoyed the widest popularity with the broad body of play-goers. But the broad body of play-goers are ashamed to confess the profound satisfaction they take in it; they begrudge the comic dramatist the double reward of praise and laughter ; and thus they make him pay the penalty of humor.

It would be easier to understand this semi-contemptuous attitude if it were shown towards the mere clowns only. Grinning through a horse-collar is not the most exalted way of earning a living—although there are worse. But the same treatment is bestowed also towards

those in whose works humor is only the out-
ward expression of serious thought. Because
the 'Fable for Critics' was full of fun, many
readers in 1849 did not discover that it was the
acutest criticism to which our young American
literature had until then been subjected. Perhaps no mask is more difficult to penetrate than
the jester's, and no disguise is more effective
than the cloak of humor. Just as Shylock was
long acted as a comic part, so 'Don Quixote' was
long accepted as a jest-book; and no part of
Mr. Ormsby's introduction to his spirited translation of the masterpiece of Cervantes is more
illuminative than the pages in which he sketches for us the successive stages of the discovery
that 'Don Quixote,' so far from being a mere
piece of fooling, is really one of the wisest books
of the world. In like manner his boisterous out-
bursts of gigantic fun, always extravagant and
exaggerated, often tasteless and obscene, veil
the knowledge and the wisdom of Rabelais.

It is not easy to suggest a philosophical explanation for the kindly condescension which
the world is wont to bestow on the humorist.
The condescension is kindly, even if it be semi-
contemptuous, and there is no suggestion of an-
imosity in it. Humor evokes little or none of
the hatred that wit so often arouses. And there

is a kind of wit of which it is well to be distrustful, for it is dangerous. This is the scoffing, girding wit which, to use George Eliot's phrase, debases the moral currency. The persiflage of Voltaire was often inspired by honest convictions; but there are writers on the newspapers of New York who have cultivated a wit not unlike Voltaire's, but with even less of sincerity in it, soiling whatever it touches—corroding and disintegrating.

There is no affinity between this sharp and envenomed wit and true humor—sometimes broad, perhaps, but always cheerful and hearty, wholesome and antiseptic. Nor is the doubt awakened by the bitter wit the cause of the public attitude towards the joyous humorist. For that we must seek deeper. Having no desire to lose myself in the mists of metaphysics, it is perhaps sufficient now to suggest that we seem to have an intuitive feeling that laughter is less elevating than weeping. Mr. Lecky thinks that a man of cheerful disposition, having enjoyed a tragedy and a farce, will admit that the pleasure derived from the former is of a higher order than that derived from the latter, and therefore, although mere enjoyment might lead him to the farce, a sense of its nobler character inclines him to the tragedy.

In other words, we intuitively feel a master-piece of tragedy to be superior to the master-piece of farce; we admit it to be higher in kind. From this intuitive belief may be deduced the reason why our attitude towards humor is semi-contemptuous. It is the reason for this intuitive belief that it would be interesting to have elucidated. Why does a laugh strike many of us as a thing unseemly in itself, and therefore to be apologized for? Admitting with Mr. Lecky that most of us feel that humor is inferior to pathos, that the tear is superior to the smile, what is the basis of this feeling? what is its scientific foundation?

Whatever its cause, this feeling is as potent to-day in the United States as it was in France in the days of Rabelais, or in Spain in the days of Cervantes. And the very strangest of its effects now, as then, is that it blinds us to the other merits of a writer who may amuse us. Though we enjoy the fun he gives us, we set him down as a fun-maker only; and when a man makes us laugh abundantly we refuse to look into his writings to see if they do not contain more than mere mirth. There is no more striking example of this injustice than one now before our eyes.

We have to-day here in the United States as

a contemporary a great humorist, who is also
one of the masters of English prose. He is
one of the foremost story-tellers of the world,
with the gift of swift narrative, with the certain
grasp of human nature, with a rare power of pre-
senting character at a passionate crisis.   There
is not in the fiction of our language and of our
country anything finer of its kind than any one
of half a dozen chapters in 'Tom Sawyer,' in
'Huckleberry Finn,' in 'Pudd'nhead Wilson.'

Partly because his fiction is uneven, and is
never long sustained at its highest level of excellence, partly because he has also written too
much that is little better than burlesque and
extravaganza, but chiefly because he is primarily a humorist, because he is free from cant and
sham pathos, because he does not take himself
too seriously, because his humor is free, flowing,
unfailing, because his laughter is robust and contagious and irresistible, because he has made
more of our scattered English-speaking people
laugh than any other man of our time—because
of all these things we do not see that in all fiction, since the single footprint on the shore fell
under the eyes of the frightened Crusoe, there is
no more thrilling moment than that when the
hand of Indian Joe (his one enemy) comes slowly within the vision of Tom Sawyer, lost in the

cave ; we do not see that no one of our American novelists has ever shown more insight into
the springs of human action or more dramatic
force than is revealed in Huck Finn's account
of the Shepherdson-Grangerford feud, and of
the attempt to lynch Colonel Sherburn ; we do
not see that it would be hard to select from all
the story-tellers of the nineteenth century a
scene of immeasurable pathos surpassing that
in ' Pudd'nhead Wilson ' when the wretched
Chambers knowingly sells his own mother
" down the river."

When we find that the man who wrote these
chapters, and so many more only a little less
marvellous in their vigor and their truth, is set
down in most accounts of American literature
as a funny man only, when we see him dismissed with a line or two of patronizing com-
ment, as though Mark Twain were only a newspaper humorist, a chance rival of John Phœnix
or Artemus Ward or Orpheus C. Kerr as a ven-
der of comic copy, then we have it brought
home to us that humor is a possession for which
the possessor must meet the bill.   Mr. Clem-
ens, having more humor than any one else of
his generation, has had to pay a higher price.

(1894.)

ON PLEASING THE TASTE OF THE PUBLIC

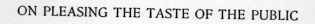

ON PLEASING THE TASTE OF THE PUBLIC

Two lines of the prologue for the opening of Drury Lane Theatre, which Dr. Johnson wrote to be spoken by his former pupil, David Garrick, still linger on our lips as a familiar quotation:

> The drama's laws the drama's patrons give,
> And we that live to please must please to live.

This pair of rymes is characterized by the robust common-sense which at once limits Johnson's criticism and gives it its chief value. Common-sense kept the man who could thus compact a simple truth into a striking couplet from giving to his assertion an extension not warranted by his own long-continued observation of the methods and the motives of men of letters. An absence of this caution has led later writers to ascribe the broad success of this or that author to the skill with which this or that author has gauged the popular taste at the moment of publication, artfully preparing his literary wares to meet a widespread demand which he has shrewdly foreseen.

This is a most unsatisfactory and a most unscientific attempt to explain away what seems often inexplicable — the interest sometimes shown by the book-buying public in the writings of an author whose works are not esteemed by his fellow-craftsmen. As it is hard to prove a negative I will not maintain that no author has ever been clear-sighted enough to guess at the probable duration of the next swing of the pendulum; but I am certain that the lucky hits of this sort must be very far between, and that any author who should rely mainly on his ability to guess at the kind of book the public was going to thirst after six months or a year later would be very likely to go hungry himself.

And I venture to believe also that there is a fallacy concealed in the phrase which speaks of "the taste of the public," for it assumes that there is a public,—*one* public having a taste in common with all its members. I am inclined to think that, so far from there being only one public, the number of publics having widely divergent likes and dislikes is indefinite, not to say infinite. These smaller publics are no two of them of the same size; and no doubt the membership of some of them is too limited for an author to hope to make his living by pleasing it.   There are in fact as many different publics as there are separate authors; and there must be, since no two writers ever made precisely the same appeal to their readers.   No two leaders in literature ever had exactly the same set of followers.   The admirers of Byron when he burst forth first had been many of them the admirers of Scott; but the two circles have not the same radius; and they are intersecting and not concentric.

The broad reading public, to which a popular author is supposed to address himself, is really rent in twain by the differences of its disputes over literary principles.   Just as a man must take either the Hebraic view of life or the Hellenic, to use the distinction that Matthew Arnold borrowed from Heine, just as he must be either an Aristotelian or a Platonist, whether he knows it or not, so he is also (perhaps from inquiry and conviction, but more probably from native temperament) either an Ancient or a Modern, either a Classicist or a Romanticist, either an Idealist or a Realist.   The standards are opposed and the conflict is irrepressible.   Whoever enlists under one of these banners is ready with the torch to torture those who volunteer to uphold the other. The very acrimony of these discussions is all the evidence any one can demand before being assured that the public is not one, single, and indivisible.

The public is really but a congeries of warring factions; and sometimes these factions are representative of the degree of development to which those who compose it have attained. Each, as it rises a step higher in the scale of civilization, naturally despises that which remains below on the plane it has just abandoned, and it is in turn detested by that over which it boasts its new superiority. Probably a similar state of affairs is visible wherever there is progress; those who are going to the front looking back with contempt on those who linger in the rear — a contempt which is repaid with frank and justifiable hatred. Perhaps as apt an illustration of this as any now available may be found in the present state of affairs existing among the vast body of men and women who are fond of the game of whist.

In Dr. Pole's calm and scientific discussion of the 'Evolution of Whist, a Study of the Progressive Changes which the Game has passed through from its Origin to the Present Time,' we are told that the development of whist has had four periods. In the first of these the player relied chiefly on his master-cards and his trumps, following suit with any one of his low cards; and this Dr. Pole calls the Primitive Game. In the second stage the game was raised into a really intellectual pastime by Hoyle and his followers, and long whist gave way before short whist. The Game of Hoyle was the basis of the development taking place during the third period, during which there was evolved the Philosophical Game, indissolubly connected with the names of Clay and 'Cavendish.' The fourth period is that of the Latterday Improvements, in which the American Leads have been adopted with other concomitant devices of like delicacy and subtlety.

As it happens there is a department of literature in which the development is singularly similar to the evolution of whist, and in which we can also declare four chronological periods, the one following the other and flowering from it. This is the art of fiction. In the beginning fiction dealt with the Impossible — with wonders, with mysteries, with the supernatural; and these are the staple of the 'Arabian Nights,' of Greek romances like the 'Golden

Ass,' and of the tales of chivalry like 'Amadis of Gaul.'   In the second stage the merely Improbable was substituted for the frankly Impossible; and the hero went through adventures in kind such as might befall anybody, but in quantity far more than are likely to happen to any single man, unless his name were Gil Blas or Quentin Durward, Natty Bumppo or d'Artagnan.   Then in the course of years the Improbable was superseded by the Probable; and it is by their adroit presentation of the Probable that Balzac and Thackeray hold their high places in the history of the art.   But the craft of the novelist did not come to its climax with the masterpieces of Balzac and of Thackeray; its development continued perforce, and there arose story-tellers who preferred to deal rather with the Inevitable than with the Probable only.   Of this fourth stage of the evolution of fiction perhaps the most salient examples are the 'Scarlet Letter' of Hawthorne and the 'Romola' of George Eliot, the 'Smoke' of Turgeneff and the 'Anna Karénina' of Tolstoi.

The four stages of whist are thus shown to have each its parallel in the four stages of fiction.*   The Primitive Game of Dr. Pole is not

* One of the editors of the Chicago *Dial* has sug-

simpler or more rudimentary than the tale of the Impossible. The Game of Hoyle is closely akin to the story of the Improbable. The Philosophical Game can be matched fitly with the novel of the Probable. The Latter day Improvements of Dr. Pole have a rigorous logic which assimilates them to the most modern form of fiction in which the Inevitable deductions are made from the characters presented.

"We have noticed four steps or stages marking the progress, and producing four varieties of game, all really whist, but whist in different stages of development," says Dr. Pole, and his words can be applied absolutely to the four varieties of fiction also. "The later forms have, indeed, grown out of the earlier ones, but have not necessarily extinguished or abolished them"—and this is true of fiction too. "The admirers of any late step are perfectly justified in showing its superiority to the one before it, but there is room enough in the world for both to continue to exist side by side"; and it is from this lofty attitude of broad toleration thus recommended by Dr.

gested that mention should here be made of the fact that "there is, and has always been, a fifth kind of fiction, corresponding to the variety of whist known as Bumblepuppy."

5

Pole that certain American critics have departed when they commented harshly on the amazing predilection certain British critics had declared for the more primitive forms of fiction. The novel-readers who prefer tales of the Impossible or of the Improbable resemble the whist-players who prefer the Primitive Game, which, so Dr. Pole informs us, is still " played by enormous numbers of domestic players, who find incidents enough in it to amuse them for hours together. And though many of them would doubtless be able to learn and to enjoy a more intellectual form, there is no reason why it should be thrust upon them, or why they should be calumniated for adhering to their innocent form of entertainment. It is probable that they follow fairly the general mode of play in the infancy of the game."

We all see that it was in the infancy of fiction that it dealt with the Impossible and in its boyhood that it began to attempt the Improbable. Although the liking for the Impossible still survives among children, and is likely to survive among them always, I am inclined to think that it is almost dead among men and women who have attained their majority. The bulk of the novel-readers of this last decade of the nineteenth century are either in the

second stage of development or in the third;
they have been wearied by the exploiting of
the Impossible, but they are not yet ready to
enjoy the discussion of the Inevitable; and
they do not care much whether the incidents
of the stories they lounge through negligently
are doubtfully Improbable or actually Probable.   But there is a certain portion of the
public which takes its fiction seriously, which
respects the art of narrative, which sees the
possibilities now open before the novelist, and
which holds the story-teller up to the highest
standard.   This portion of the public—wel-
coming warmly the fiction which gives the
most truthful interpretation of life—is steadily
gaining in numbers and in influence.

I fear that its swifter increase is not a little
retarded by its own intolerance towards the
novel-readers who yet delight in the Primitive
Game.   This attitude is easy to understand,
but none the less is it unfortunate.   "We may
take it for granted that, whatever may be the
exclusive notions of the select whist aristocracy, there will always be a large democratic
body who will please themselves as to what
sort of game they will play," says Dr. Pole,
very pertinently.   "The amiable lady who be-
gins by playing out her aces, or the pleasant

club-member who leads his lowest card from
five, ought not to be upbraided for bad play.
All that should be said is that they play varieties of the game differing from that recommended in 'Cavendish's' latest edition." In
like manner the late Professor Boyesen should
not have berated Mr. Andrew Lang for pre-
ferring Mr. Haggard's gory romances to Tolstoi's more serious discussions of human experience. The American critic should have contented himself with pointing out that his British colleague liked the Primitive Game better
than the Latterday Improvements. And really
it was unreasonable in Professor Boyesen to
expect that Mr. Lang should appreciate the
new American Leads, either in literature or in
life.

Any movement forward by the more intelligent is like the sending ahead of skirmishers,
and we have no right to expect to find the
main body of the army close at the heels of
the advance-guard. The most we can hope
is that the ground taken by the few pio-
neers yesterday shall be held in force to-day.
Generally any improvement in taste makes its
way slowly, and the bulk of the public must
always lag long behind the keener intellects
that delight to spy out a new land for them-

selves. In New York City, for instance, the last thirty years have seen a most extraordinary increase in the popular appreciation of music.

Toward the end of the sixties Mr. Theodore Thomas and his orchestra played every summer night in the old Central Park Garden, and the programme was made up largely of medleys from Offenbach's operettas and of dance-music. Owing to Mr. Thomas's increasing efforts to give better and better music as he educated the New York concert-goer, and owing also to the labors of Dr. Damrosch and Mr. Seidl, there is now perhaps no city in the world where more music of the highest class is heard in the course of the year than in New York, and none where it is more delicately enjoyed. The finest of Wagner's music-dramas are not now too solid fare for the subscribers of the Metropolitan Opera-house, who no longer find any satisfaction even in the most expensive performance of sugary trifles like the 'Lucia' of Donizetti.

But though the subscribers of the Metropolitan Opera-house have lost their liking for 'Traviata' and for 'Trovatore,' the occasional experiments of other opera companies in other New York theatres and in opera-houses in other cities of the Union seem to show that there are perhaps as many music-lovers as ever who have advanced just far enough to understand and enjoy these simple favorites of former days. The opera-goers of this class are like the whist-players who stick to the Primitive Game, or the novel-readers who revel in romances of the Improbable. And I have no doubt that if a young conductor possessing such shrewdness and force as Mr. Thomas revealed, should give summer-night concerts in New York, placing on his programme dance-tunes and medleys from operettas, he would have now quite as large a following as Mr. Thomas had thirty years ago; and in time he could slowly lead on this portion of the public to the acceptance of music demanding a more careful appreciation.

There is ready at hand yet another example of the ease with which a portion of the public can be educated to have a relish for the finer forms of art. It was in the sixties that Mr. Theodore Thomas began his elevating work here in New York; and it was in the seventies that the American magazines began to seek for a fresher and a richer pictorial embellishment, a search which slowly brought into existence the illustrated monthly due to the loving co-operation of the editor, the artist, the engraver, and the printer. The best of these sumptuous publications, having gradually created the taste by which they were estimated, attained to an enormous circulation—a fact which might seem to prove them to be precisely "the kind of periodical that the public wants."

Yet early in the nineties we saw the appearance of a swarm of cheaper monthlies, filled with process-blocks from photographs; and some of these slight magazines also attained to an enormous circulation. But as the success of these new periodicals affected only a little (if at all) the sale of the older and solider magazines, it is obvious that "the kind of periodical that the public wants" is a question to which there are now two answers. In other words, while one segment of the reading circle has been led to develop a liking for the more substantial merits of the established magazines, another segment is attracted by the cheap tawdriness of the more flimsy novelties. And it is quite within the bounds of possibility that an inventive editor might now devise a third form of periodical which should also attain to an enormous circulation without interfering with the profits of either class of monthly now most in favor; he would only be proving the existence of a third segment of the reading circle.

So I return to the assertion made in an early paragraph of this essay: there is really no such entity as *the* public. There is *a* public ready to welcome everything which is good in its kind; and there are as many publics as there are different kinds of good things. Few of us are so limited in our likings as to belong to one public only. The extreme Wagnerite is often warmest in praise of a captivating waltz by Strauss; and the extreme veritist can acknowledge the charm of a romantic fantasy of Stevenson's. Perhaps a reader of extraordinary catholicity might belong almost to all the different publics.

Some of these publics are very large indeed and some of them are very small. 'Hamlet,' for example, appeals to almost every type of play-goer, while the performance of Ibsen's 'Ghosts' pleases only a chosen few. In general, of course, the higher up the pyramid is cut, the smaller will be the area of the cross-section—'Hamlet' being one of the rare works which are so nearly universal as rather to bisect the pyramid than to cut across it. When one has once grasped firmly the idea that the people at large are massed in a pyramid, one layer above the other, with the most intelligent at the apex, one cannot but see the futility of all assertions that " the public wants to be amused," and " the public wants sensation and excitement," and "the public does not want analysis and disquisition." There is a public that wants to be amused ; and perhaps the larger portion of this public wants sensation and excitement, and does not want analysis and disquisition. But there is a public also which does want analysis and disquisition, and does not want sensation and excitement. There is a segment of the reading circle with the keenest relish for airy fantasy and for delicate humor. There is another segment hungry for the naked truth. There is yet another which has no real liking for knowledge of itself, and which therefore likes to hear over and over again the old outworn tales and to listen again and again to old outworn rymes of *love* and *dove*, of *heart* and *part*.

This diversity of public taste has always existed — except perhaps in the compact community of Athens. In the prologue he wrote for the third performance of one of his comedies, Terence denounced the foolish public because at the first performance it was all excitement over an exhibition on the tight-rope which was to follow, and because at the second performance the theatre emptied itself suddenly in the middle of the play when a rumor ran around the house that there were going to be gladiators elsewhere in the neighborhood. (If I may open a parenthesis here, I should like to drop the query as to whether Gresham's Law may not be as potent in art as it is in finance, the inferior product driving out the superior, as the bloody shows of the arena in Rome finally extinguished the Latin literary drama.)   In England, under Elizabeth, the wooden theatres in which Shakespeare's sublimest tragedies were acted served on other days of the week as a ring for the sport of bear-baiting.   In the early part of the nineteenth century in London, when Sarah Siddons and John Philip Kemble were in the plenitude of their powers, they played often to the bare benches of Drury Lane, while the same night Covent Garden would be packed with people eager to behold a real elephant take part in a spectacular pantomime.   The elephant and the bear-baiting and the gladiators, each in their turn, pleased that part of the public which was still playing the Primitive Game—to use Dr. Pole's phrase—and which therefore was wholly incapable of understanding the Philosophic Game, so to speak, of Mrs. Siddons, of Shakespeare, and of Terence.

And yet that portion of the public which clings to the Primitive Game has at least one fine quality: it is perfectly sincere. It is not a humbug or a sham. It knows what it likes, and it is not ashamed of its prejudices. It makes no pretence of regard for the more advanced art it is unable to appreciate. It is frank and outspoken in its conviction that Hawthorne is slow and Turgeneff dull; and it makes no effort whatever to conceal its opinion that Ibsen is tiresome and that Mr. Howells is colorless. It is wholly without the snobbishness which induces not a few of those readers who really most enjoy the romances of Mr. Rider Haggard to pretend that they prefer the novels of Mr. George Meredith merely because there was once a Meredith cult among the cultured.

I am inclined to believe that the position of that portion of the public which retains its primitive taste in literature is often misrepresented and even more often misunderstood. For one thing, this portion of the public is composed of plain people who are not only sincere themselves in their literary likes and dislikes,

but are also swift to detect insincerity in the
authors who seek to interest them. They revolt at the slightest hint of condescension.
They insist on being taken seriously;—and this
is why the ingenious tales of accomplished lit-
erators often fall flat, while hundreds of thousands were sold of the sensational stories of
" Hugh Conway," who was not at all a man of
letters.

Here we find a possible explanation for a
problem which has puzzled more than one generation of literary critics—why do the writings
of certain authors have an immense vogue, although these authors are seen to be without the
really great qualities? Is success in literature
only a lottery? Is the general public a fool
then, easily to be led by the nose? As there is
no effect without a cause, there must be a reason
for the popularity which sometimes seems to us
unaccountable. The real explanation of the welcome which was bestowed on the ' Proverbial
Philosophy' of the late Martin Farquhar Tupper, for example, or on the novels of the late
E. P. Roe, is to be sought in the sincerity of
these two writers. Neither was in any way a
charlatan. Both of them gave the public the
best they had in them; and, as it happened,
they thus voiced the unformulated feelings

of the segment of the reading circle to which they themselves belonged. So far from writing *down* to the public taste, as they were accused of doing, they were, in fact, writing *up* to the taste of the portion of the public that welcomed their works. By their own birth and bringing up, both Mr. Tupper and Mr. Roe were in a measure representative of the "plain people," as Lincoln phrased it; and they could not help taking the plain people's point of view. This the plain people recognized promptly; and the writers had their reward on the spot. Their writings lacked the permanent qualities of literature, no doubt, and that is why their vogue was temporary only.

More accomplished men of letters than either Mr. Tupper or Mr. Roe have not taken this point of view naturally, and thus they have failed to voice the feelings of the very segment of the reading circle they hoped to please. Indeed, I doubt if any author who has tried to guess at the taste of the public that he might flatter it, has ever made a hit satisfactory to himself; and I am certain that no author who really despised his audience, as more than one author may have pretended that he did, has ever really pleased those to whom he made

his appeal thus cynically. It happens that I
have met at one time or another many of the
novelists and dramatists of France, of England,
and of America—those whom the critics delight
to honor and those also at whom the criticas-
ters joy to gird; and the quality which the latter class seemed to me to have most abundantly was earnestness. They believed in their own
work, and they were doing it as well as in them
lay. Their success was due to the fact that
their best corresponded absolutely with the
ideal of a certain segment of the reading circle
or of a certain proportion of the play-goers.
In other words, and to use another of the keen
phrases attributed to Lincoln, these popular
novelists and dramatists were producing "just
the kind of thing that a man would like who
liked that kind of thing." And that is why they
met with a far wider success than the far cleverer
and far more accomplished men of letters whose
merits might be vaunted by all who had themselves so far progressed in literature as to appreciate the Latterday Improvements, as Dr. Pole
calls them. It is only now and again that there
comes a rare writer able to delight at once his
brethren of the craft and the plain people also;
and he does this not by trying to please the
public, but rather by expressing himself and

by doing always the best he knows how.   His segment of reading circle subtends a very wide angle because his art is as firm as his outlook on our common humanity is broad.

(1895.)

ON CERTAIN PARALLELISMS BETWEEN THE ANCIENT AND THE MODERN DRAMA

[This paper was originally contributed to ' Classical Studies in Honor of Henry Drisler,' published in 1894 by the Columbia University Press.]

ON CERTAIN PARALLELISMS BETWEEN THE ANCIENT AND THE MODERN DRAMA

FOR the man of letters who has let his classical studies lapse on leaving college, and who takes them up again a score of years later, there are compensations, as I have recently discovered by personal experience. What the man of letters who does this has lost is incalculable and irrecoverable, no doubt, and what he may gain is but little indeed and of small worth — yet it is something if it be only a renewed freshness of view. And it is indisputable that this is the chief gain — this ability to look at old texts from new standpoints, and to interpret the life and the literature of the past by the aid of a deeper knowledge of the life and the literature of the present.

The vital principles of any art are always the same, and they subsist through the ages essentially unchanged, however much they may seem to be modified superficially by the varying fashions of succeeding generations. Of no art are the fundamental laws more absolutely fixed than are those of the drama. When, therefore, one who has given his attention for twenty-five years to the modern stage returns to the study of the ancient theatre, he might fairly be expected now and again to note points of contact between the old and the new.

A knowledge of the manners and customs of the players and the playwrights of Paris and London and New York enables the student to understand better than he could otherwise the manners and the customs of the players and the playwrights of Athens and Rome. When any one having an acquaintance with the modern playhouse inquires into the practices of the ancient theatre, he cannot but remark in the older plays features which are often supposed to be the sole property of the most recent playwrights. In the Greek theatre, for instance, it is not difficult to discover that the dramatist was generally careful to provide an "exit-speech" whenever an important character left the stage; nor is it hard to detect among the plays of Euripides more than one specimen of the "star-piece." Though there may be no Greek equivalents for these technical terms, the things these words denote existed in Greece none the less.

The terminology of the contemporary theatre is precise and copious, although it has not as yet been recorded fully in any dictionary of the English language, or even in any technical vocabulary of its own. A "star-piece," for example, is a play so devised as to display all the histrionic powers of the performer of the chief part. Certain of Shakespeare's plays are obviously "star-pieces": 'Hamlet,' for one, and 'Richard III.,' for another; and so is the 'Medea' of Euripides. Medea is not only the "star-part," but the other characters of the play are little more than mere "feeders"— that is to say, they exist, not for their own sake, but solely for their relation to Medea; and they speak, not to reveal themselves, but solely to afford occasion to Medea to express herself fully and at length and under the strain of the most poignant emotions. The character played by the protagonist is all-important, and the characters played by the deuteragonist and by the tritagonist are all of them subordinated and effaced. It is known that there were strolling companies of performers in Greece and in the Grecian colonies, as there have been of late years in Great Britain and the United States

(Haigh's 'Attic Theatre,' p. 43); and to give a fairly satisfactory performance of the 'Medea' only one great actor was needed.

A renowned Athenian protagonist could "go on the road" with the 'Medea' as certain of pleasing the multitudes who would flock to see him act in the theatres of the smaller Greek cities as Madame Sarah-Bernhardt is now certain to delight the audiences who fill the playhouses of all the larger towns of the whole world to behold her suffer and die in 'La Tosca.' Nor has M. Sardou contrived 'La Tosca' more adroitly for this special portability than Euripides composed the 'Medea.' Euripides is like M. Sardou in more ways than one; in his exceeding cleverness, for instance, in his dramaturgic dexterity, in his mastery of theatrical device, in his predilection for women as his chief characters.

"It is stated," so Mr. Haigh reminds us in his admirable volume on the 'Attic Theatre' (p. 76), citing the authorities for the statement, "that Sophocles was accustomed to write his plays with a view to the capacities of his actors." No one who has investigated the methods of the great modern dramatists would venture to dispute this assertion; and it would be easy to adduce reasons for thinking that Eurip-

ides did what Sophocles was accused of doing.*
An analysis of the 'Medea' has convinced me
that in composing this play Euripides was, in
all probability, carefully "fitting"—to use the
technical term of the theatre of to-day—some
Athenian actor by whose extraordinary histrionic ability he wished to profit, just as M. Sardou, in composing 'La Tosca,' fitted Madame
Sarah-Bernhardt, just as Molière, for that matter, certainly fitted Mademoiselle de Molière
when he was writing 'Le Misanthrope,' and just
as Shakespeare possibly fitted Master Bur-
bage when he was writing 'Hamlet.' And while
'Hamlet' and 'Le Misanthrope' are the masterpieces of their authors, the 'Medea,' again, is
rather like 'La Tosca,' in that it owes its permanent popularity to the histrionic opportunities it affords. After all, what we go to the
theatre to see is—in the final analysis—acting.
Whatever we may like in the library, in the
theatre we prefer the plays which give most
scope to the actors.

"Exit-speech" is the name given to the final
words spoken by a character before he leaves
the stage after an important scene. Nowadays an exit-speech is generally a point of

* Compare Aristotle, 'Poetics,' 9 (1451 b 38).

one kind or another, rhetorical or jocular. In
Shakespeare's time the exit-speech very often
ended with a couplet, the rymes of which
were signals to the groundlings to be ready
with their applause. In the great period of
the Spanish drama, which was contemporary
with the Elizabethan drama of England, the
utility of the exit-speech was perfectly understood, and in the 'Arte nuevo de hacer come-
dias,' in which Lope de Vega laid down pre-
cepts for the guidance of practical dramatists, he
advises the 'prentice playwright thus : "Adorn
the end of your scenes with some swelling
phrase, with some joke, with lines more carefully polished, so that the actor at his exit
does not leave the audience in ill-humor." In
the Greek drama the exit-speech is frequent.
In the ' Medea,' again, Jason's final words at
the end of the stormy scene with his wife have
all the characteristics of the exit - speech
(619–22) :—

> ἀλλ' οὖν ἐγὼ μὲν δαίμονας μαρτύρομαι,
> ὡς πάνθ' ὑπουργεῖν σοί τε καὶ τέκνοις θέλω·
> σοὶ δ' οὐκ ἀρέσκει τἀγάθ', ἀλλ' αὐθαδίᾳ
> φίλους ἀπωθεῖ· τοιγὰρ ἀλγυνεῖ πλέον.

[Yet I call the gods to witness that I seek to help
thee in all things and our children as well ; but thou

carest nought for favors but spurnest thy friends in
wilfulness, and for this thou shalt have the greater
sorrow.]

An exit-speech also of the most approved
type is Medea's, when she leaves the stage
after the marvellously pathetic scene with her
children, and after the messenger has declared
the success of her scheme to kill her rival
(1244–50):—

ἄγ᾽ ὦ τάλαινα χεὶρ ἐμὴ, λαβὲ ξίφος,
λάβ᾽, ἕρπε πρὸς βαλβῖδα λυπηρὰν βίου,
καὶ μὴ κακισθῇς, μηδ᾽ ἀναμνησθῇς τέκνων
ὡς φίλταθ᾽, ὡς ἔτικτες · ἀλλὰ τήνδε γε
λαθοῦ βραχεῖαν ἡμέραν παίδων σέθεν,
κᾄπειτα θρήνει · καὶ γὰρ εἰ κτενεῖς σφ᾽ ὅμως
φίλοι γ᾽ ἔφυσαν, δυστυχὴς δ᾽ ἐγὼ γυνή.

[Come, thou daring hand of mine, grasp, grasp the
sword! Put thyself at the start of a miserable life;
and become not weak nor give thought to thy children, how dear to thee, how thou didst give them
birth! But forget thy children for this brief day, at
least, and then bewail them; for even if thou goest
about to slay them, they were born into thy affection,
and I—a wretched woman!]

The complement of the exit-speech is the
device now known as "working up an entrance."
A leading actor likes to have his coming before
the audience for the first time in the play care-

fully prepared and plainly announced, so that expectancy may be aroused and recognition may follow at once upon his appearance on the stage. Every play-goer can recall instances of the ingenuity with which the modern play-wrights have been able to work up the entrance of important characters; there is no better example, perhaps, than the first appearance of the heroine in 'Adrienne Lecouvreur,' the drama devised for Rachel by Scribe and M. Legouvé. Now this working up an entrance for the chief persons of the play was far more needful in the Greece of old than it is in the Paris and in the New York of to-day, for the Grecian theatres were many times the size of ours, and the actors wore masks which hid their features, and—so far as I know, at least — there were no programs to aid in identification. Therefore, we find that the Greek dramatists were very careful to work up the entrance even of unimportant characters. In the 'Medea,' once more, after the prologue in which the nurse declares herself, no person of the play comes on unannounced by some one already on the stage; and the appearance of Medea herself is worked up quite in the most modern manner, her loud bewailings off the stage being expounded by the nurse.

The fact is that the psychology of the theatrical spectator is very much the same in all climes and in all ages. The New York boy who perches in the upper gallery of the Broadway Theatre, however deficient in intelligence when compared with the citizen of Athens seated on a marble bench in the beautiful theatre of Dionysus, has needs like his in so far as they are both play-goers. Both demand clearness above all things; both desire not to be left in doubt as to what is going on before them. For a man at the play, understanding is the condition precedent of enjoyment.

It is greatly to be desired that some classical scholar should familiarize himself with the modern theatre, so that he might approach the study of the drama of antiquity with a full understanding of the present methods of the same art. Much of the value of Patin's ' Tragiques Grecs ' is due to his knowledge of the French theatre and to his constant use of the modern stage for comparison with the ancient. In this, as in other respects, Professor Mahaffy has followed in Patin's footsteps. But no one has yet done for the Greeks what the late M. Goumy attempted to do for the Latins—to explain the past in terms of the present. It would be too much to say that M. Goumy, who died before he had half finished his task, was wholly successful in finding modern equivalents for ancient experiences. But 'Les Latins' is a volume to be read with refreshment and stimulation; and it is good for us to be told that Cæsar's 'Commentaries' was really what we Americans might call "a campaign autobiography," and that Cicero did not deliver his orations as they have come down to us, but "asked leave to print," so to speak, that he might polish his periods at leisure.

Though I have neither the scholarship nor the time to undertake the explanation of the ancient drama by the modern theatre in the method I have suggested, I can furnish a few additional instances of parallelism perhaps not unworthy of record. The likeness of the Greek tragedy, with its appropriate music, its slow and stately movement, and its use of local legend, to the Wagnerian music-drama has been dwelt on sufficiently; and, even as I penned these paragraphs, I found in the second number of the new *Revue de Paris* an essay on the specific resemblances of 'Die Walküre' to the 'Antigone.' But less attention has been drawn to a more recent return to Greek principles of playmaking, Ibsen's presentation of only the culminating point of the plot, and his concentration of all the interest of the action into its compact climax, in which the 'Œdipus Rex' itself is scarcely more skilfully contrived than is 'Ghosts.'

It may seem most irreverent to suggest a similarity between a masterpiece of humor like the 'Frogs' and an amusing modern burlesque like the 'Adonis,' in which Mr. Dixey parodied the peculiarities of Mr. Henry Irving, much as some Athenian comedian must have mimicked the mannerisms of Euripides; but nevertheless the similarity of the two pieces is striking enough. Indeed, the difference between 'Adonis' and the 'Frogs' is due mainly to the fact that the author of 'Adonis' was only a clever comic playwright, while the author of the 'Frogs' happened also to be a great poet— just as it is also his poetic power which gives Euripides his immeasurable superiority over M. Sardou. In the 'Frogs,' for example, Bacchus, in the costume of Hercules, is like a modern actor in classic attire, crowned with the very latest style of stove-pipe hat; and when Bacchus appeals to his priest sitting officially in front of the stage, he is not unlike the comedian of our time who holds a colloquy with the leader of the band. I confess that the comic servant, Xanthias, in the 'Frogs,' complaining that he is not allowed to complain, reminds me of the comic servant, Greppo, in the ' Black Crook,' also involved in mysterious adventures which he does not understand.

I wonder whether or not it was a tradition of the Grecian theatres that the performer who played Xanthias, or any other comic servant of the sort, should wear many garments of contrasting colors, superimposed one on the other so that he might excite the laughter of unthinking spectators by removing them one by one. This " business" is traditional with the Second Grave-digger in the ' Hamlet' of Shakespeare, and with Jodelet in the ' Précieuses Ridicules' of Molière; and it is derived probably from some forgotten farce of the Middle Ages, which in turn was possibly descended from some Roman pantomime. Visible jests of this kind are very long-lived, and no doubt many of them passed over from the Latin *fabulæ Atellanæ* to the Italian *commedie dell' arte*.

For the adapted comedies of Plautus and Terence, with abundant Roman allusions flowering out of Grecian plots, more or less skilfully transplanted, there are many modern parallels. It is not at all uncommon to see on the modern English-speaking stage a French or a German play, roughly twisted into conformity with the conditions of British or American life. They may be amusing, like Mr. Augustin Daly's later adaptations from the German, or they may be exciting like some of his earlier adaptations from the French; yet there cannot but be always an obvious and inevitable unreality in any drama merely decanted in this fashion. While the comedies of Plautus may thus be likened, not unfairly, to the modern English localized arrangements of foreign plays, the skill with which the Latin dramatist presented the every-day life of the Roman household and market-place suggests that his comedies may also be compared with the amusing and broadly sketched pieces in which Mr. Harrigan has most comically set before us the characteristics of the polyglot population of New York.

Perhaps no peculiarity of Greek comedy has seemed stranger to latter-day commentators than the parabasis; and yet to discover modern equivalents even for this is not difficult. I think it is even possible to derive from our own experience the reason why the earlier dramatists were moved to make use of this device. The parabasis—so Müller describes it in the 'History of the Literature of Ancient

Greece (i., p. 401)—is "an address of the chorus in the middle of the comedy"; and in it "the poet makes his chorus speak of his own poetical affairs, of the object and end of his productions, of his services to the state, of his relation to his rivals, and so forth." Then the chorus sings a lyrical poem, and recites in trochaic verse "some joking complaint, some reproach against the city, some witty sally against the people." It is this second part of the parabasis that Professor Mahaffy, in his 'History of Greek Literature' (i., chap. xx.) likens to the "topical song" of the modern burlesque, "which is always composed on current events, and has verses added from week to week, as new points of public interest crop up."

The first part of the parabasis, wherein the poet makes the chorus his own mouthpiece, and addresses the audience almost in his own person, is very closely akin to the Elizabethan prologue, in which the dramatist discussed the play about to be performed, in which occasionally he abused his rivals, and in which he sometimes vaunted himself. And here the prologue, like the parabasis, performed a useful function; for as the psychology of the play-goer changes but little through the ages, so also the psychology of the playwright is substantially the same in Periclean Athens and in Elizabethan London. Above all things, the spectator wants to be able to understand what he is seeing, and the dramatist wishes to have his work seen from his own point of view. The playwright is glad to have the right of rising to a personal explanation. Nowadays the novelist and the poet can declare in a preface the code by which they wish to be judged. The dramatist cannot avail himself of this privilege; and the prologue is the only preface he is permitted. If he cannot get the ear of the public for an explanation outside of his work, he must perforce make this explanation a part of the work itself, placing it either at the beginning, as Ben Jonson did, or in the middle, as did Aristophanes.

The frequency with which the prologue was made to perform this function is well brought out in 'A Study of the Prologue and Epilogue in English Literature,' (by "G. S. B.," London, 1884), wherein it is shown that the prologue was of real service to Ben Jonson, and that it was useful even to Dryden, although he had already other means of reaching the public ear. The prologue and the epilogue still accompanied new plays at the end of the eighteenth

7

century, although they had ceased to have any close connection with the pieces before and after which they were spoken. It is obvious that the prologue and epilogue in Sheridan's plays, for example, are mere survivals of an outworn fashion.

Yet even in this century, when the dramatist can call on the journalists to publish abroad any declaration he may desire to make, there are occasions when the temptation to expound his own theories of his art inside the work of art itself are too strong to be overcome. In the 'Antony' of the elder Dumas, in the fourth act, there is a discussion between Eugène and the Baron de Marsanne about Romanticism; what is this but a prose parabasis cut into dialogue? And in the 'Denise' of the younger Dumas, the analysis of the thesis of the piece by Thouvenin — in what manner does this differ essentially from the parabasis? So frequent has been the use of a character like Thouvenin by M. Dumas *fils*, and by certain of his contemporaries, that the French critics have been forced to find a name for this new stage-type; they call the character who explains the play a *raisonneur*. As it happens, the delivery of the parabasis is not the sole duty of the *raisonneur*, for he performs other functions of the chorus, of which multiple personality he may be supposed to be a condensation into a single person. He listens to the talk of the hero and of the heroine, taking the part of the *confidant* of French tragedy (itself a feeble substitute for the chorus of Greek tragedy); he asks the proper questions to evoke the fullest expression of the hero's and the heroine's sentiments; he is properly sympathetic; and he also serves as a speaking-trumpet for the author, being sometimes, as in 'Les Idées de Madame Aubrey,' charged with the utterance of the final moral.

To the ancient chorus and to the modern *raisonneur* there was even a medieval analogue. In the interludes—which followed the mysteries and the moralities, and which with them prepared players and play-goers for the coming of the dramatized chronicle and of the romantic drama—"not infrequently," so Symonds records in his 'Shakespeare's Predecessors in the English Drama' (p. 176), "a Doctor, surviving from the Expositor of the miracles, interpreted the allegory as the action proceeded."

(1894.)

TWO SCOTSMEN OF LETTERS

TWO SCOTSMEN OF LETTERS

I.—MR. ANDREW LANG

THE most lifelike photograph of a friend is no more than a reminder of what we have seen for ourselves, since the camera has neither insight nor imagination; a portrait by a true artist may bring out qualities but doubtfully glimpsed before, or it may even reveal depths of character hitherto unsuspected. In one of the London exhibitions during the season of 1885, amidst many a " portrait of a gentleman," there was at least one portrait of a man— nervous, significant, vital. At a glance it was obvious that the man here depicted was a gentleman and a scholar, although the picture had none of the prim propriety of the ordinary academic portrait. There was an air of distinction about the sitter, twisted around in his chair, with his frankly humorous gaze. The casual stranger whose eye might fall on the painting could not but feel that the restless attitude was inevitably characteristic, and he could not but confess the charm of a most interesting personality. And, indeed, Mr. Richmond's picture of Mr. Andrew Lang seems to me one of the most successful of modern portraits.

Perhaps the first effect it makes on the beholder is to suggest the extreme cleverness of its subject—an effect which may do an injustice to Mr. Lang, for cleverness is best as an extra, as the superfluity of him who has some quality other and better. Molière was not clever, and M. Sardou is clever beyond belief. When cleverness is all a man's having, though he make a brave show for a while, he is poor indeed. Cleverness Mr. Lang has, and a plethora of it; but he has also a richer endowment. He may be called the Admirable Crichton of modern letters ; and he is a graduate of St. Andrew's, that ancient Scottish university where the original Crichton was once a student three centuries earlier. Thence he went to Oxford, where there lingered memories of Landor and Shelley, where he took the Newdigate prize for poetry, and where in due season he was elected a Fellow of Merton, the college of Anthony Wood. Herein, I think, we may grasp the clew to Mr.

Lang's character, and to his career: he is a Scotsman who has been tinctured by Oxford, but who still grips his stony native land with many a clinging radicle.

Mr. Andrew Lang and the late Robert Louis Stevenson were for a while the two Scottish chiefs of literature. Both lived out of Scotland, yet both were loyal to the land of their birth, and loved it with all the ardor of a good son's love. Neither was in robust health, but there was no taint of invalidism in the writings of either, no hint of morbid complaint or of unwholesome self-compassion. Both were resolutely optimistic, as becomes Scotchmen. Both were critics, with sharp eyes for valuing, and with a faculty of enthusiastic and appetizing enjoyment of what is best. They had both attempted fiction, and both belong to the romantic school. In differing degrees each was a poet, and each was master of a prose than which no better is written in our language nowadays. Mr. Lang's style has not the tortured felicity of Stevenson's; its happiness is easier and less wilful. The author of 'Letters to Dead Authors' is not an artificer of cunning phrase like the author of 'Memories and Portraits'; his style is not hand-made nor the result of taking thought; it grows more of its own accord. The style of each is transparent, but while Stevenson's is as hard as crystal, Mr. Lang's is fluid like water; it flows, and sometimes it sings as it flows, like the beautiful brooks he longs to linger beside, changing with the sky and the rocks and the trees, but always limpid and delightful.

American readers, annoyed at the slovenliness of most modern British essayists, are struck by the transparent clearness of Mr. Lang's style; for though he was born north of the Tweed his pages are spoiled by no Scotticisms, and though he dwells by the banks of the Thames they are disfigured by no Briticisms. They are free from the doubtful English which has the "largest circulation in the world." A constant perusal of the fine prose of the great Frenchmen whom Mr. Lang admires and a devoted study of the great Greeks whom he loves may have helped to give his pages their indisputable ease.

In his pellucid prose, as in his intellectual alertness and in his lightness of touch, Mr. Lang is rather French than English. He is a nephew of Voltaire and a cousin of M. Jules Lemaître. As we read his graceful and nervous sentences sometimes our ear catches an echo of Thackeray's cadences; and it was in

France that Thackeray served his apprentice-
ship to the trade of author. Sometimes our
eye rejoices in the play of a humor always
lambent and often Lamb-like; and it is perhaps from Charles Lamb that Mr. Lang has
got the knack of the quotation held in solution. Like Dryden and Burke and Bagehot,
three masters of English prose, Mr. Lang
quotes abundantly and from a full memory,
and not always exactly. "Verify your quo-
tations" is not a warning that he has taken
to heart. The books from which he can draw
illustrations at will are numberless, and they
are to be found in every department of the
library. In Greek literature, and in French
as well as in English, he has the minute thor-
oughness of the scholar; but his main reading seems to have been afield, as happens
to every man who loves books, and who likes
to browse among them without let or hinder-
ance.

The equipment of a critic Mr. Lang has, and
the insight, and also the sympathy, without
which the two other needful qualities lose half
their value. There are limits to his sympathy,
and he tells us that he does "not care for Mr.
Gibbon except in his autobiography, nor for the
elegant plays of M. Racine, nor very much for

Mr. William Wordsworth, though his genius is undeniable"; but the range of his knowledge and of his understanding seems to me as wide as that of any other contemporary British critic. He is unfailing in affection for Homer, Herodotus, Theocritus, and Lucian, for Vergil and Horace, for Rabelais, Molière, and Dumas, for Shakespeare, Fielding, Miss Austen, and Thackeray, for Scott and Burns. He delights in the skittish writings of the lively lady who calls herself "Gyp," while for the psychologic subtleties of M. Paul Bourget he cares as little as does "Gyp" herself. He was prompt in praise of the author of 'King Solomon's Mines'; in fact, Mr. Haggard's tales of battle, murder, and sudden death have found no warmer eulogist than the author of 'Ballades in Blue China.'

Longfellow declared that "many readers judge of the power of a book by the shock it gives their feelings, as some savage tribes determine the power of muskets by their recoil; that being considered the best which fairly prostrates the purchaser." Mr. Lang's taste is too refined for this saying to be justly applicable to him; but he does not think the worse of a book because it tells a tale of daring-do. He is eager for a story of

> battles, sieges, fortunes . . . . .
> Of moving accidents by flood and field,
> Of hair - breadth 'scapes i' the imminent deadly
> breach.

He is quick to give a cordial greeting to a traveller's history of "antres vast and deserts idle," of "Anthropophagi, and men whose heads do grow beneath their shoulders." In other words, Mr. Lang is a romanticist to the bitter end. Broad as his sympathy is, it is not broad enough to comprehend realism. He is restive when realism is lauded. Unconsciously, no doubt, he resents it a little; and he does not quite understand it. Mr. Lang can enjoy Rabelais, and praise him for the qualities which make him great in spite of his wilful foulness; but in M. Zola Mr. Lang sees little to commend. Quite the most perfunctory essay of Mr. Lang's that I ever read was one on the author of 'L'Assommoir,' which did but scant justice to the puissant laborer who toiled unceasingly on the massive edifice of the 'Rougon-Macquart' series, as mightily planned and solid in structure as a medieval cathedral, and, like it, disfigured and defiled by needless and frequent indecencies. Tolerant towards most literary developments, Mr. Lang is a little intolerant towards the analysts. Amiel delights

him not, nor Marie Bashkirtseff either; and it
irks him to hear Ibsen praised, or Tolstoi,
though the pitiful figure of Anna Karénina
lingers in his memory. And as for Mr. Howells, it is hard to say whether it is as novelist
or critic that he irritates Mr. Lang more. Mr.
Howells once spoke of the critical essaylets
which issued monthly from the 'Editor's
Study' as "arrows shot into the air in the
hope that they will come down somewhere and
hurt somebody." Enough of them have hit
Mr. Lang to make him look like St. Sebastian,
if only he had not plucked them out swiftly,
one by one, and sent them hurtling back across
the Atlantic. Fortunately, the injuries were
not fatal on either side of the water, and there
was no poison on the tips of the weapons to
rankle in the wounds. Sensitive as most British writers are to the darts of transatlantic
criticism, it has seemed to me sometimes that
Mr. Lang is even tenderer of skin than are
most of his fellow-sufferers.

The ocean that surges between Mr. Howells
and Mr. Lang is unfordable, and there is no hope
of a bridge. There is no common standing-
ground anywhere for those who hold fiction to
be primarily an amusement and those who believe that it ought to be chiefly a criticism of

life. The romanticist considers fiction as an art, and as an art only, whilst the extreme realist is inclined to look on it almost as a branch of science. Kindly as Mr. Lang may be in his reception of a realistic book, now and then, he stands firmly on the platform of the extreme romanticists. " Find forgetfulness of trouble, and taste the anodyne of dreams—that is what we desire " of a novel, he declares in his cordial essay on Dumas. And in another paper he calls again for a potion against insomnia:

Pour out the nepenthe, in short, and I shall not ask if the cup be gold-chased by Mr. Stevenson, or a buffalo-born beaker brought by Mr. Haggard from Kakuana-land—the Baron of Bradwardine's Bear, or 'The Cup of Hercules' of Théophile Gautier, or merely a common café wineglass of M. Fortuné du Boisgobey's or M. Xavier de Montépin's. If only the nepenthe be foaming there—the delightful draught of dear forgetfulness—the outside of the cup may take care of itself; or, to drop metaphor, I shall not look too closely at an author's manner and style, while he entertains me in the dominion of dreams.

Here Mr. Lang is in accord with Mérimée, who wrote in 1865 that " there is at present but one man of genius: it is Ponson du Terrail . . . No one handles crime as he does, nor assassination. *J'en fais mes délices*." But

Mérimée's humorous exaggeration is not in accord with his own practice; however abundant in imaginative vigor his stories might be, nothing could be more rigorously realistic in treatment. Mr. Lang seems to me happiest as a story-teller when his practice departs from his theory. His longest story, the 'Mark of Cain,' is as who should say a tale by M. Xavier de Montépin, but by a Montépin who was a Scotsman, and had been to Oxford, and did not take himself quite seriously. Now, for a romanticist not to take himself seriously is to give up the fight before the battle is joined. Mr. Lang has balladed the praises of "Miss Braddon and Gaboriau," and he may be sure that these masters of sensation believed in themselves, else would they never have held thousands breathless. If an author once lets his readers suspect that he is only "making believe," instantly he loses his grip on their attention, and may as well put away the puppets, since few spectators will care to wait till the fall of the curtain.

The one fault that Mr. James found with Trollope—that "he took a suicidal satisfaction in reminding the reader that the story he was telling was only, after all, a make-believe"— Mr. Lang never commits of malice prepense;

but though he does not confess this unpardonable sin in so many words, yet his tone, his manner, his confidential approach, make the confession for him, and readers find themselves glancing up from the printed page to to see if the author has not his tongue in his cheek or is not laughing in his sleeve. And the crime is the more heinous in story-telling according to the romantic tradition than in fiction of the realistic school. Mr. James reminds us that "there are two kinds of taste in the appreciation of imaginative literature — the taste for emotions of surprise, and the taste for emotions of recognition." It is the latter that 'Barchester Towers' gratifies, and it is to the former that the 'Mark of Cain' appeals; and the taste for the emotions of surprise is not satisfied if it suspects the writer of treating tragic moments with levity, or even of being capable of such treatment. But perhaps the real reason why a public that accepted the tawdry 'Called Back' did not take kindly to the 'Mark of Cain' is that the latter story was too clever by half—a thing resented by most of those who share Mr. Lang's taste for the emotions of surprise.

Perhaps the same criticism applies to some of the stories in the collection called 'In

8

the Wrong Paradise'—to the Poe-like tale of
'A Cheap Negro,' for example.   But others
of the stories in this volume, especially the
uncanny tales of spooks and of medicine-
men, are most delicious fooling—and fooling
founded on the impregnable rock of modern
science.   What could be better in its way
than the 'Great Gladstone Myth?' — wherein
the grand old man is resolved into his elements in the fashion familiar to students of
sun-myths.   Equally amusing, and quite as
pregnant in suggestion, is the description of
the poor souls who found themselves each
'In the Wrong Paradise'—the scalped Scotchman dwelling with the Apaches in their happy
hunting-grounds, and the wretched cockney
esthete desperately out of place in the For-
tunate Islands of the Greeks.   And in the
volume of pleasant papers on 'Books and
Bookmen' there is an eery tale of painful
and humorous misadventure in 'A Bookman's
Purgatory.'   Akin to these in method, and
even superior to them in charm, is the story
of 'Prince Prigio,' which of all Mr. Lang's fictions I like best, unhesitatingly proclaiming
it the most delightful of modern fairy-tales
since the 'Rose and the Ring'; and if any
one should tell me that he found no fun in

the awful combat between the Firedrake and
the Remora, I should make answer that such
an one, waking or sleeping, does not deserve
ever to receive as a gift, or even as a loan,
the seven-leagued boots, the cap of darkness,
or the purse of Fortunatus—all properties of
fairy - lore with which Prince Prigio was duly
accoutred.

From fairy-land to the doubtful region of
folk-lore is no seven-leagued stride, and Mr.
Lang is master in both territories. He stands
ready to trace the kinship of Barbarossa and
Barbe-bleue, and to insist that neither is a
child of the sun. In defence of his theories
Mr. Lang is armed to give battle to Profess-
or Max Müller and his men; and they find
him a redoubtable opponent, in no danger of
putting off the heavy armor of scholarship
because he has not proved it, and never without a smooth stone in his scrip to cast full at
the forehead of his adversary. Lowell has
protested against that zeal which seeks to explain away every myth as a personification of
the dawn and the day. " There's not a sliver
left of Odin," he declared:

> Or else the core his name enveloped
> Was from a solar myth developed

> Which, hunted to its primal shoot,
> Takes refuge in a Sanskrit root,
> Thereby to instant death explaining
> The little poetry remaining.
> Try it with Zeus, 't is just the same;
> The thing evades, we hug a name;
> Nay, scarcely that—perhaps a vapor
> Born of some atmospheric caper.

Against the philologic school of mythologists of whom Professor Max Müller is the chief, Mr. Lang has led a revolt in behalf of an anthropological explanation of those habits, customs, beliefs, and legends for which the upholders of the sun-myth theory provided an etymological interpretation. Mr. Lecky tells us that invariably with increased education the belief in fairies passes away, and "from the uniformity of this decline, we infer that fairy-tales are the normal product of a certain condition of the imagination; and this position is raised to a moral certainty when we find that the decline of fairy-tales is but one of a long series of similar transformations." Inspired by McLennan and Professor Tylor, and following Fontenelle, Mr. Lang has given battle to those who maintain that the descriptions of the elemental processes of nature developed into myths, and who accept a personification

of fire, storm, cloud, or lightning as the origin
of Apollo and his chariot, Thor and his ham-
mer, Cinderella and her slipper, and B'rer Rabbit and the tar-baby.

In the stead of the arbitrary interpretations
of the philologists, wherein scarcely any two
of them are agreed, Mr. Lang proffers an explanation derived from a study of the history
of man and founded on the methods of com-
parative anthropology. He turns to account
the evolution of humanity from savagery to
civilization, and he examines the irrational
beliefs and absurd customs which survived in
Greece even in the days of Pericles by the aid
of a study of the beliefs and customs of savage tribes still in the condition in which the
ancient Greeks had once been. Thus he is
ready to see in the snake-dance of the Moquis
of Arizona a possible help to the right understanding of a similar ceremony described
by Demosthenes. He seeks to show that in
savagery we have " an historical condition of
the human intellect to which the element in
myths, regarded by us as irrational," seems
rational enough. Further, he urges that as
savagery is a stage through which all civilized
races have passed, the universality of the
mythopœic mental condition will explain not

only the origin, but also the diffusion throughout the world, of myths strangely alike one to another.

That this ethnological hypothesis has gained general acceptance, and placed the philologic theory on the defensive, is due almost altogether to the untiring advocacy of Mr. Lang. His views have been presented modestly but firmly and incessantly. He has prepared the case himself, examined the witnesses, and summed up for the plaintiff. And he is an awkward antagonist, quick-witted and keen-sighted, and heavy-laden with the results of original anthropological investigation. He has scholarship in the old sense of the word ; and to this he adds the advantage of a memory which retains every pertinent fact accumulated during omnivorous reading over a marvellously wide range of subjects. Most disinterested scholars have now accepted either as a whole or in part the theory Mr. Lang has set forth.

Of the scholarship which forms the solid basis for Mr. Lang's scientific inquiry he has given abundant evidence in his nervous prose translations of the 'Odyssey' and the 'Iliad' done in partnership with friends, in his refined rendering of the 'Idyls' of Theocritus, and

in his fresh and fragrant version of that other
idyl, 'Aucassin and Nicolette.' His translations reveal an unusual union of scholarly ex-
actness with idiomatic vigor; they are graceful—almost the rarest quality of a translation
—and they are unfailingly poetic. Perhaps
an enforced quaintness, and an occasional
insistence on an archaic word, seem almost
like affectation, but this may be forgiven in
the charm and the felicity of the rendering as
a whole. The secret of this charm is to be
found, I think, in Mr. Lang's attitude towards
the authors he translates. To him Homer,
and Theocritus, and the old man who sang
of 'Aucassin and Nicolette,' are still living,
and their works are alive. Scholar as he is,
his interest is never grammatical or philo-
logical, but always literary and human. He
never regards these writings as verse to scan,
or as prose to parse, but poetry to be enjoyed.

As it happens, Mr. Lang has attempted no
long translations in verse, but some of his
briefer metrical attempts are almost as happy
as Longfellow's, than which there can hardly be higher praise. No doubt the carrying
over of a lyric from one language to another
is an easier task than the transferring of an
epic, but nevertheless it is a feat many a

minor poet has failed to accomplish. The difficulty lies in the double duty of the translator to present the thought of his original and to preserve the form, not sacrificing the spirit, and at least suggesting the atmosphere. Mr. Lang has given us the most satisfactory version of Villon's 'Ballade of Dead Ladies' (although Rossetti attempted it earlier), and of Clément Marot's 'Brother Lubin' (although both Longfellow and Bryant severally essayed it, neglecting to retain the ballade form).

In his brightsome 'Ballades in Blue China,' and in his brilliant 'Rhymes à la Mode,' Mr. Lang shows his mastery of the accomplishment of verse, and his skill in that department of poetry which seems easy and is beset with danger. Voltaire tells us that difficulty conquered in whatsoever form of art is a large share of the merit; and neither in sonnet, nor ballade, nor other fixed form of verse, has Mr. Lang shirked any difficulty. If the game is worth the candle, Mrs. Battle is right in insisting on the rigor of the game. In his freer stanzas Mr. Lang has sometimes something of the singing simplicity of Longfellow and Heine, where the music of the verse sustains the emotion. In 'Twilight on Tweed'—

A mist of memory broods and floats,
    The Border waters flow:
The air is full of ballad notes,
    Borne out of long ago,

and in the 'Last Cast,' the angler's thoughts
wander to the rivers he has never fished, and
then go back to the streams of Scotland
again:

Unseen, Eurotas, southward steal,
    Unknown, Alpheus, westward glide,
You never heard the ringing reel,
    The music of the water-side!

Though gods have walked your woods among,
    Though nymphs have fled your banks along,
You speak not that familiar tongue
    Tweed murmurs like my cradle-song.

My cradle-song—nor other hymn
    I'd choose, nor gentler requiem dear
Than Tweed's, that through death's twilight dim
    Mourned in the last Minstrel's ear.

Mr. Lang has taken for an epigraph Molière's *Ce ne sont point de grands vers pom-
peux, mais de petit vers*, yet he has at times
the gift of lofty lines. It is only fair to judge
a poet by his highest effort. In the case of
the present poet these seem to me to be two

sonnets on Homer, of a sustained and noble elevation.   For love of Homer's heroine Mr. Lang has written his longest poem, 'Helen of Troy,' a brevet-epic.

> The face that launch'd a thousand ships
> And burnt the topless towers of Ilium

holds its fascination still across the centuries. Nor is "Sweet Helen," as Faustus calls her, the only lady of Mr. Lang's affections.   He has a wealth of platonic love for many a fair dame (in poetry), and for many a damsel in distress (in prose).   I doubt if he would deny his devotion to Beatrix Esmond, for whose sake the author of the 'Faithful Fool' (a comedy once performed by Her Majesty's Servants) broke his sword before his king.   I question whether he would not admit an affection for Mrs. Rawdon Crawley, *née* Sharp, a green-eyed lady who once acted Clytemnestra at the Gaunt House theatricals.   I know that he confessed a fondness for Manon Lescaut, a young person of reprehensible morals, who lightly sinned in France and then died happily in Louisiana.   And I think that he is ready to boast of his liking for Miss Annie P. Miller of Schenectady, New York, an American girl who was known to her intimates as "Daisy," and who died in Rome after an imprudent visit to the Colosseum by moonlight.

Mr. Lang has the same frank and sturdy love for literature that he has for some of its captivating female figures. No reader of his could be in doubt as to his ceaseless and loyal study of Homer and Theocritus, of Rabelais and Molière, of Shakespeare and Thackeray. And in sports, too, his tastes are as wholesome and as abundant as his predilections in letters. He cherishes the cricket of Oxford and the golf of St. Andrews; he follows with equal zest trout-fishing and book-hunting. Than this last there is indeed no better sport; and the poetic author of 'Books and Bookmen' has proved his interest in the bees of De Thou as well as in those that made the honey of Hymettus. The original Crichton, we may remember, sent an epistle in verse to Aldus Manutius, the great printer-publisher of Venice.

Mr. Lang is at his best when he writes about the Scots and about the Greeks of old, for these he knows and loves; and perhaps he appears to least advantage when he is writing about the American writers of to-day, since these he neither likes nor cares to know— and unsympathetic criticism is foredoomed to

sterility. The native Americans Mr. Lang is
most familiar with are the red men, and he is
fonder of them, I fancy, than he is of the pale
faces who have built towns by the banks of
the streams over which Uncas and Hard-Heart
skilfully propelled their birch - bark canoes.
It might have been better, therefore, had he
not laid himself open to Mr. Fiske's rebuke
for the "impatient contempt" with which he
chose to speak of a man of Lewis H. Morgan's
calibre; and if he had not permitted himself
a doubtfully courteous attack on Professor Boyesen. And a more careful understanding of
American literary history would have saved
Mr. Lang from that farewell to Poe, in the
'Letters to Dead Authors,' in which the
author of the 'Raven' is hailed as "a gentleman among *canaille !*"—surely as strange an
opinion as one can find in all the long annals
of criticism.

'Letters to Dead Authors' is one of the
minor masterpieces of letters, the keenest and
cleverest volume of playful criticism since the
'Fable for Critics' was published twoscore
years ago, as that in its turn was the brightest
book of the kind since 'Rejected Addresses.'
But I am afraid to linger over this delightful tome for fear I may laud it extravagantly.

The 'Epistle to Mr. Alexander Pope,' a marvel of parody with many lines as good as the one which tells the poet that

Dunces edit him whom dunces feared!

the letter to " Monsieur de Molière, Valet-de-Chambre du Roi," with its delicious suggestion that if the great and sad French humorist were alive to-day he might write a new comedy on *les Molièristes ;* the communication to Herodotus, with its learned fooling ; the missive to Alexandre Dumas, with its full current of hearty admiration and enjoyment — these and many another I dare not dwell on, because, as I read in the letter to W. M. Thackeray, "there are many things that stand in the way of the critic when he has a mind to praise the living." Quite as welcome as these are some of the essays in epistolary parody to be found in 'Old Friend.'

Of necessity every man has the defects of his qualities, and the very success of Mr. Lang's briefer essays tends to prevent his attempting longer labors. He gets most out of a subject which may be treated on the instalment plan, when every portion is complete in itself, and yet unites with the others to form a complete whole. A book like

'Letters to Dead Authors,' which is avowedly
a collection of separable essays, has not only
a broader outlook but also a stronger unity
than the pleasantly discursive volume on Oxford, for example. A collection of Tanagra
figurines, however, is in no wise inferior in
interest to a colossal statue; art has nothing
to do with mere bulk, nor has literature. Mr.
Lang cultivates to best advantage ground
which can most easily be cut into allotments.

It is to be noted also that despite his extreme multifariousness there are certain seg-
ments of life and of literature in which Mr.
Lang takes little interest or none. Though
he once wrote a poem on General Gordon,
and though he is ever chaffing Mr. Gladstone,
it is obvious that he cares not for the con-
tentions of politics; and apparently he cares
as little for the disputes of theology, although
he did write a chance article on 'Robert
Elsmere.' For art, music, and the drama he
reveals no natural inclination. We may guess
that it has been his fate to serve as art-critic,
toiling in the galleries yearly; but we can
discover no signs of any real understanding
of art, either pictorial or plastic, nor of any
aptitude for it. Of music he says almost
nothing, and he seems to know as little about

it as we know about the song the Syrens sang. And as for the acted drama, I am afraid that he is a heretic, even as Lamb was heretical in regard to the performance of Shakespeare's plays. I hesitate to assert, though I am inclined to believe, that to him 'As You Like It' and 'Much Ado About Nothing' are comedies to be read in the fields or by the fireside, rather than stage-plays to be acted before the footlights.

(1893.)

II.—MR. ROBERT LOUIS STEVENSON

THE news of the death of Robert Louis Stevenson in that far-off Pacific isle, removed by half a continent from his native Scotland, gives a sudden shock to all who care for our later literature; and it has left us, I think, with a sense of personal loss, as though he had died with whom we had held delightful intercourse in the past, and with whom we could hope to have many another stimulating talk in the future. This feeling is doubled and far deeper in those of us who had the privilege of knowing Stevenson, even if our acquaintance with him were as slight as mine—and I can treasure the precious memory of but a single long afternoon on the same sofa with him, in the dingy back smoking-room of the Savile Club, one dismal day of a London summer nearly ten years ago. Chiefly we talked of our craft, of the art of story-telling, of the technic of play-making. I remember distinctly his hearty praise of Mark Twain's 'Huckle-

berry Finn,' and his cordial belief that it was
a great book, riper in art and ethically richer
than the 'Tom Sawyer' of which it is the
sequel. I recall the courtesy and the frankness with which he gave me his opinion of a
tale of mine he happened to have read recently. Frankness, indeed, was a constant quality
of his conversation; and perhaps his spoken
word was fresher and freer than his written
lines—it could not but be less premeditated.
With a very strong individuality, there was no
pose in his manner, no affectation, no airs and
graces. He looked unlike other men, with his
tall thin figure, his long thin face, his nervous
thin hands. As one's eyes first fell on him
one felt that he was somebody, and not anybody at random. If one had dropped into
ta ith him by chance in a train or in a
do s waiting-room, one could not have
resi d the impress of his personality. He
talk well, although not perhaps with the
spon aneous many-sidedness of his friend
Flee ing Jenkin (whom he introduced as
Coc hot in his own essay on 'Talk and
T s'). He talked well, standing up square-
l nst the other party to the conversation,
hol his own stoutly, expressing his views
in st ightforward fashion, with no beating

9

about the bush, no questing of epigram, no strain of phrase-making. He talked well, as he wrote well, because he had something to say, and because he had taught himself how best to say it.

In the writing of the author, as in the talk of the man himself, perhaps the two salient qualities were vigor and variety. The vigor every one has felt who chances to have read a single book of Stevenson's—and who of us, having read any one of them, has not sat himself down to read them all? The variety is equally evident if we look down the long list of his works—and the list is really very long indeed, when we remember that the books on it were written, all of them, by a dying man, who finally departed this life before he was fifty. He was a poet of distinction, although not of high achievement. Although no single one of his poems has been taken home to the hearts of the people of his speech, yet 'A Child's Garden of Verses' is as unlike any rymes of earlier poets as any volume of verse of this last quarter of the nineteenth century. He was a writer of travel-sketches, and again he revealed the same originality, and he was able to describe 'Edinburgh,' his boyhood's home, with the same freedom from

staleness, the same eschewal of the commonplace, that gave freshness to 'Silverado Squat-
ters ;' while in 'Travels with a Donkey' and
'An Inland Voyage' he achieved a detach-
ment of the man from his circumstances
unattempted by anybody before, excepting
only the author of 'Walden.'   He was a biog-
rapher and a literary critic, and although his
life of 'Fleeming Jenkin' is the least successful of his works, being marred by a hint
of a patronizing manner entirely unbecoming
towards a man of the character and accomplishment of "The Flamer," still the task was done
in workmanlike fashion ; and Stevenson's other
sketches of authors in his 'Familiar Studies
of Men and Books,' and elsewhere, are free
from this defect.   It is to be noted here that
he was one of the rare British critics capable
of appreciating Walt Whitman with sanity,
while another American, Thoreau, was perhaps almost the strongest of all the influences
which moulded him—quite the strongest after
Scott, I think.   He was an essayist, and
among the most piquant and individual of his
day, an essayist of the race and lineage of
Montaigne, of Lamb, and of Lowell, interested
in life as much as in literature, seeing for himself, always inquiring and always acquisitive,

having philosophical standards of his own, and using them to measure men and manners, and yet never intolerant, though ever sincere. He was a dramatist at least one of whose plays, 'Deacon Brodie,' was fairly successful in withstanding the touchstone test of the actual theatre; yet it must be admitted that his dramas, written, all of them, in conjunction with Mr. W. E. Henley, have rather the robustious manner of that burly writer than the commingled delicacy and force of Stevenson's other work. And, lastly, he was also a story-teller.

It is as a story-teller that he won his widest triumphs; it is as a story-teller that he is most likely to linger on the shelves of our grandchildren's libraries; it was as a story-teller that he revealed his greatest variety. First and last he tried his hand at four kinds of fiction. In the 'New Arabian Nights' with its sequel, the 'Dynamiter,' he revived the tale of fantasy with an inventive ingenuity unequalled certainly since Poe published 'Tales of the Grotesque and the Arabesque.' In the 'Strange Case of Dr. Jekyll and Hyde,' and in 'Markheim,' he gave us strongest stories of introspection and imagination since Hawthorne's 'Scarlet Letter' and

'Marble Faun.' In 'Kidnapped' and in 'David Balfour' and in the 'Master of Ballantrae' he presented us with the most vivid and actual of Scotch romances since Scott came home from vacant exile to die at Abbotsford. And in the 'Wrecker' and certain of its fellows he tried, not without a large measure of success, to varnish with sheer art the vulgar detective-story, and to give a tincture of literature to the tale of crime committed and the secret ferreted out at last. And even now, though it has been easy to show that as a teller of tales Stevenson's versatility has thus four phases, 'Treasure Island' has to be left out of the account, simply because it refuses to classify itself with the others—perhaps because it prefers to take its chances with 'Robinson Crusoe.'

Stevenson had his theory of fiction, and his practice was like his preaching—which is another proof of his originality. In the evolution of the modern novel from the primitive romance, in the progress first from the Impossible to the Improbable, and then from the Probable to the Inevitable, he refused to go to the end.

He preferred the Improbable to the Inevitable. He was a romanticist to the backbone,

a reactionary, so those of us think who most
relish in literature the essence of actual life.
But though he fought for his own hand, and
defended his own doctrine stanchly, with characteristic good faith he tried to understand
the point of view of those with whom he con-
tended.   Himself liking the dramatic novel,
as he called it, the bold romance wherein is
set forth the strife of passionate character
against passionate character, he did not ap-
prove of Mr. Henry James's habit of keeping
the *scène-à-faire* behind closed doors.   Yet in
his reply to Mr. James's paper on the 'Art of
Fiction,' a reply which he modestly entitled
'A Humble Remonstrance,' he combated the
views of the author of 'Daisy Miller' with the
utmost courtesy; and in a postscript to the
same paper he recorded his dissent from what
he called the "narrow convictions" of Mr.
Howells; but he seized the occasion to declare
the author of 'Silas Lapham' to be "a poet, a
finished artist, a man in love with the appearance of life, a cunning reader of the
mind."

Being a Scotsman, Stevenson was nearer to
the American than the Englishman can be,
and he had a quicker willingness to understand the American character.   As a Scots-

man, also, he had keener artistic perceptions
than an Englishman is likely to have.   He
was not only a born story-teller, as Scott was,
but he was also a master of the craft, a loving,
devoted, untiring student of the art, which
Scott was not.   He never attained to the
mastery of form which Guy de Maupassant
derived as a tradition from the French classics;
his stories are often straggling.   And he had
not the relish for fresh technicalities which is
one of Mr. Rudyard Kipling's peculiarities.   I
remember Fleeming Jenkin telling me how
his sons, who had sailed a boat from their
earliest youth, were sorely puzzled by the impossible manœuvres of the ship in 'Treasure
Island,' and how they came to their father
despairingly to declare that "this never happened, did it?   It couldn't, could it?"

Not only these deficiencies have been dwelt
on, but the absence has been pointed out of
what is known as the "female interest" in
his stories; and it is a fact that almost the
only satisfactory and enticing petticoats of Mr.
Stevenson's draping are in 'David Balfour.'
But these defects are as naught against the
narrative skill of Stevenson, his unfailing fer-
tility of invention, his firm grasp of character,
his insight into the springs of human nature,

and, above all, his contagious interest in the tale he is telling.

Whether it is a tale he is telling, or a drama with its swift sharp dialogue, or an essay rambling and ambling skilfully to its unseen end, the style is always the style of a man who has learnt how to make words bend to his bidding. He writes as one to whom the parts of speech must needs obey. He had a picked vocabulary at his command, and he was ever on the watch for the unexpected phrase. He strove incessantly to escape from the hackneyed form of words, and cut-and-dried commonplaces of speech—and no doubt the effort is evident sometimes, although the instances are rare enough. There is at times, it is true, more than a hint of preciousness, but he never fell into the self-consciousness which marred many of the late Mr. Walter Pater's periods. 'Prince Otto,' written obviously under the influence of Mr. George Meredith, had more of these aniline patches, as it was also the feeblest of his fictions. The open letter on Father Damien, for example, had a sturdy directness of statement which suggested Walt Whitman again.

The impression of mere dilettante idling which one may get at first from some of the earlier essays is evanescent. As Mr. James put it, much as Stevenson " cares for his phrase, he cares more for life, and for a certain transcendently lovable part of it." And herein Mr. James saw " the respectable, desirable moral." To me, at least, there was no need to seek a moral between the lines, for was not Stevenson a true Scotchman, and could he ever forget the chief end of man? Only a Scotsman could have written the ' Strange Case of Dr. Jekyll and Mr. Hyde,' as only a New-Englander could have written the ' Scarlet Letter.' There is an inheritance from the Covenanters and a memory of the Shorter Catechism in Stevenson's bending and twisting the dark problems of our common humanity to serve as the core of his tales.

It is curious that a writer so independent as Stevenson and so various should have been tempted so often into collaboration; but it is a fact that no man of letters of our time and our language has taken more literary partners. With Mr. W. E. Henley he composed at least four plays, and they are to be set down rather to Mr. Henley's credit, as I have suggested, than to Stevenson's. With Mrs. Stevenson he wrote the ' Dynamiter ;' and with her son, Mr. Lloyd Osbourne, he told three tales, the ' Wrong

Box,' the 'Wrecker,' and the 'Ebb-Tide,' in
which we find a more open humor than in his
other stories. But, as those only know who
have themselves collaborated in good faith, it
is always impossible to disentangle the contri-
bution of one partner from that of the other,
if, indeed, there has been not a mere mechan-
ical mixture, but a true chemical union. Whatever associates Stevenson had now and again,
he was the senior partner always, and it was
his trade-mark that warranted the goods of
the firm.

(1894.)

ASPECTS OF FICTION

ASPECTS OF FICTION

I.—THE GIFT OF STORY-TELLING

WHENEVER the annalist of English literature shall record the history of the year 1894, one of the most curious items he will have to set down in his account cannot but be the sudden success achieved in fiction by a mature practitioner of another art. To take all hearts by storm, Trilby had only to appear, and no sooner did she show herself than hundreds of thousands of readers lay prostrate at her incomparable feet. Irresistible as was Mr. Du Maurier's charming heroine, and however acceptable the tale of Trilby's misadventures may be as a reproduction of actual life, it is not a masterpiece of narrative art. Delightful as it is, full as it is of the freshness of youth and of the joy of living, it could easily be torn to pieces, as a story merely, were any critic hard-hearted enough for the hateful task. No one knows better than Mr. Du Maurier that his unpretentious romance is not *savamment filé*, as he might say himself. He has not studied fiction as an art diligently from his youth up; and it was late in life, and almost by accident, that he discovered his ownership of the gift of story-telling.

The gift of story-telling! This it is which Mr. Du Maurier has, and which he obviously did not know he had, or he would have revealed it earlier in his career. It is this gift of story-telling which Mr. Du Maurier has unexpectedly found himself to possess in a high degree that enables him so to enchant us with his tale that we overlook all the evidences of his inexpertness as a maker of romances. It is this native faculty of narrative which the writer of fiction must needs have as a condition precedent to the practice of his craft, and without some small portion of which the conscious art of the most highly trained novelist is of no avail.

This gift of story-telling can exist independently of any other faculty. It may be all that its possessor has. He might be wholly without any of the qualifications of the literator; he might lack education and intelligence; he might have no knowledge of the world, no experience of life, and no insight into character; he might be devoid of style, and even of grammar;—all these deficiencies are as nothing if only he have the gift of story-telling. Without that, he may have all the other qualifications and still fail as a writer of fiction. With that, even though without them, he may make sure of an audience whenever and wherever he shall choose to take up his tale.

In so far as the gift of story-telling exists independently, it is like the ability to make an effective speech, the knack of writing an actable play, the power of acquiring money; and its possession is no proof whatever that the possessor is abler than his fellows except in that one direction. That a man succeeds in anything is evidence that he had not mischosen his calling; that whatever his general intelligence may be, and however slight it may be, he has at least a full share of the special intelligence needed in the art in question (be that only the humble art of making money). Here we have an explanation of the surprise which has shocked us often on meeting the maker of an immense fortune when he revealed himself as a man of no great intelligence. It accounts for the sharp disappointment we have felt on finding that the musician, the painter, the tragedian of high rank in his profession may be a man of no more than ordinary intellectual force.

A chance remark of a distinguished French comedian first suggested to me this simple explanation. I had met a member of the company, and I had found him almost stupid, although as a performer he was more than acceptable; and I asked my friend how this could be, that so dull a man could be so good an actor. He shrugged his shoulders and smiled, and answered: "Why not? It is just the same in the other arts." I was forced to admit that I had known musicians also who had nothing to recommend them but their music. "Painters too," he returned. "Look at M——, the greatest painter we have, and he's an old chump!" for so I venture freely to render the untranslatable French phrase *vieille ganache*. "It is the same in all the arts: to succeed in any of them one needs the intelligence of that art—one doesn't need any other intelligence."

A further consideration has led me to make a threefold classification of successful actors—first, those who have the histrionic faculty and nothing else; second, those who are intelligent, and who make their intelligence a substitute for the natural gift; and third, those few who,

besides being born actors, are also men of intellect and character. Charles Lamb's friend
Munden may be taken as the type of the actor
who is an actor only. Munden must have been
a great comedian; but it is only as a comedian
that he was great; in the ordinary relations of
life he was a very ordinary man. Macready,
on the other hand, is an instance of the success with which a deficiency of the native histrionic faculty can be supplemented by force
of character and by general intelligence. Macready was not a born actor; he was a made
actor. Lewes—than whom there is no shrewder
English dramatic critic—declares his belief that
Macready would have made his way to the
front either at the bar or in the Church quite
as well as he did on the stage. But who could
imagine Munden in any other calling than the
comedian's?

A large majority of the actors of any time
belong to the first of these classes; they act
because " it is their nature to "; their readings
and their gestures are right more often than
not from unconscious intuition, not from any
reason they could give. Smaller and yet always well represented is the second division,
men and women of little natural endowment
for the theatre, making up for this deficiency

by exceeding carefulness, by conscientious study, by sheer force of determination. These are the performers who are coldly praised as "scholarly." In London I once asked a friend who really understands the theatre what sort of an actor so-and-so was. "So-and-so?" he answered; "he is a most scholarly actor, understanding his art thoroughly; but sooner than see him act, I'd rather be all alone by myself in a dark room!"

The third class, consisting of those who have intellect and character and culture as well as a natural gift for their vocation, is as rare on the stage as it is in the studio or in the library; it must always be very rare everywhere. The typical actor having this double endowment was David Garrick, who was at once the first tragedian of his time and the first comedian, who was the foremost manager and one of the leading dramatists, who wrote delightful light verse, and who held his own as a talker with the best men of The Club, and who was altogether the marvel of the stage. In our own days it is not difficult to designate actors who have not only the histrionic faculty in a very high degree, but who have also, like Garrick, a full share of culture and character and intellect. Mr. Joseph Jefferson here in America,

M. Coquelin in Paris, Herr Barnay in Berlin—these are among the first names that now come to mind.

A triple classification like this here attempted for actors can be made for all other artists—for painters, for sculptors, and for architects, for orators, for poets, and for dramatists. All fall into the three divisions—those with the special temperament, those with general ability, and the scanty few who have both the general ability and the special temperament. Turner, for example, was born to be a painter, and he knew nothing but how to paint; Washington Allston made himself a painter by indomitable perseverance; while Michael Angelo had ability of many kinds, and in a high degree. To turn from one art to another, Sheil was a born speech-maker, and Whitfield had the same gift of eloquence, but neither of them had anything to say which has survived; while Burke was the profoundest political thinker of his century, yet he had so little of the natural gift of the orator that his delivery of the speeches we still study emptied the House of Commons. Strangely infrequent is the power of impressing an immediate audience with words that will also abide after the interest of the occasion has departed. Daniel Webster achieved this triumph more than once, though he never equalled the pregnant simplicity of Lincoln's Gettysburg speech, which carried away the listening thousands on the battle-field then, and now is cherished in the hundreds of thousands of memories.

Among the dramatists the second of these three classes is very small indeed. In the making of a play to please the broad public (to which the dramatist must always appeal), temperament counts for far more than culture. Without the inborn dramaturgic faculty the ablest man of letters finds himself absolutely at a loss. This dramaturgic faculty is wholly distinct from literary ability; and it sometimes is to be found in the possession of men having little or no tincture of literature. And this is why critics, trained to appreciate purely literary qualities, so often fail wholly to understand the success of a popular play, the literary defects of which are too obvious; this is why they are so often forced to wonder at the failure of the brilliantly written comedy of a man of letters who happens to be without the dramatic temperament. It is the born playwright who has interested the broad public at all times; he has interested it none the less when he chanced also to have literature. As a substitute for

the specific gift literary art was inadmissible,
but as a supplement it was welcome. It is
style alone that survives; and so most of the
plays of the past which had the widest popularity have sunk out of sight, and their makers'
names are forgotten.

Lamb calls Heywood a "prose Shakespeare;" and of all the early Elizabethan
dramatists none was more acceptable to the
play-goers of the period than Heywood; he
had the dramaturgic faculty, he was a born
playwright, but it was only now and again
that he rose to the level of literature. Ben
Jonson sought to make up for his lack of the
natural gift by scholarship and energy and
toil; and in most cases he had his labor for
his pains, and he took his pay in contempt for
those who refused to be amused by his hard
work. Shakespeare had the native endowment, and he was the best "Shakescene of
them all"—the most popular playwright of
his time. That he was the hack-dramatist of
his theatre, patching up old plays to tempt
the groundlings, and knowing every trick of
the trade and up to every device of the craft,
did not prevent him from being also the greatest of English poets. But it is not the abiding
beauty of his verse, it is not his profound

insight into human recognized character, it is his native gift of play-making by contemporary play-goers which keeps a third of his comedies and tragedies on the boards now nearly three hundred years after his death.

Just as one man succeeds in the theatre because he is a born playwright, despite his deficiency in all other qualities, so another man wins his way as a poet because he is a born lyrist. If he have but the gift of song, we have no right to expect from him anything else. From a songster it is absurd to demand thought; if he but give us melody, that is enough. A poet may be a literary virtuoso of incomparable technic, like Théophile Gautier, for example — a surpassingly skilful artist in words, and quite incapable of anything fairly to be called an original thought. His verse may be a marvellous instrument for the reproduction of tones and tints and delicate shades of sensation and emotion, and he himself may have a small mind and a little soul. There are those who have proclaimed Wordsworth to be a thinker as well as a poet, but they would be daring indeed who should set up such a claim for Tennyson, than whom the literary history of England records no more accomplished master of the art of verse.

Yet the late poet-laureate eagerly assimilated much of the best thought of his time, and thus nourished his stanzas and gave them substance and solidity. But the French poet who was Tennyson's contemporary and rival was less receptive; it might almost be said that Victor Hugo was as impervious to thought as he was to humor. He was a singer of lyrics, a painter of pictures in rhyme; just a poet and nothing else. As one of the acutest of recent French critics, M. Jules Lemaître, has put it, compactly, "A man for whom Robespierre, Saint-Just, and even Hébert and Marat, are giants, for whom Bossuet and De Maistre are odious monsters, and for whom Nisard and Mérimée are imbeciles, this man may have genius, but, beyond all question, genius is all he has." And yet no one has been ampler than M. Lemaître in praise of Hugo as a poet pure and simple. The author of 'Odes et Ballades' was the greatest of French lyrists, making a stubborn and rebellious language soar and sing, and doing this easily, abundantly, unceasingly.

It was the gift of poetry that Hugo had, and Tennyson, just as Munden had the gift of comedy, as Sheil had the gift of eloquence, as Turner had the gift of painting—just as Mr.

Du Maurier has the gift of story-telling. No doubt Mr. Du Maurier has other qualities also —a pleasant humor, for example, and broad sympathy; but these would all be of little avail if he had not also the gift of story-telling. The possessor of this precious birthright seems to divine many of the secrets of the art of narrative almost intuitively, and he has no difficulty in holding our attention while he spins the yarn. However inexperienced he may be, he is rarely ineffective; and at his first attempt he often does easily and without effort what those who have not the gift must take thought to accomplish, and attain only after striving and straining.

The gift of story-telling all the most popular romancers of the time possess and must possess or else they would not have won popularity. And sometimes this gift is all their having. Sometimes they own little or no more, having neither wit nor wisdom, neither style nor psychology—possessing, indeed, no general ideas even about the art they practise with applause. This is how it comes to pass that more than one of the purveyors of popular fiction of our day has made a sorry spectacle of himself when he took it upon himself to discourse upon his own art and to discuss its secrets. The public had read his books because he was a born teller of tales, but for criticism of craftmanship he had no gift, and in attempting it he was merely giving himself away.

As one glances down the long and interesting history of fiction, one can readily pick out the names of novelists belonging to one and another of the three classes. And yet the writer who has the gift of story-telling and nothing else, who has neither style nor humor nor the ability to create character, who is a spinner of yarns only, has no staying power; however immense his immediate popularity may be, he sinks into oblivion almost as soon as he ceases to produce. Perhaps there are no more typical specimens of the story-teller pure and simple than the late Ponson du Térrail in France (the historian of the misdeeds of Rocambole), and the late "Hugh Conway" in England (the author of 'Called Back'). Perhaps it would be invidious to point out any living writers of tales belonging in this class; and yet the temptation to name names is wellnigh irresistible.

In the second division, containing those without the native faculty and yet with ability which they impress as a substitute for the gift, it is probably perfectly fair to include Dr.

Johnson. 'Rasselas' reveals no natural endowment for the pursuit of fiction; it is the result
of main strength misapplied. Perhaps also
Diderot is to be included in this class, for the
author of 'La Réligieuse' had the gift of story-
telling as little as he had the dramaturgic
faculty. It may be unfair to Diderot, whose
intelligence was alert and swift, to link his
name with that of Johnson, who moved pon-
derously; and yet they are both examples of
the inadequacy of intellect alone as an equipment for the practice of an art without some
portion, however slight, of natural endowment.
For the spinning of yarns, the intelligence
alone will not suffice.

The two great contemporaries Boccaccio
and Chaucer had both the gift of story-telling
in fullest measure; they were also among the
most accomplished and most intellectual men
of their time. Boccaccio was a scholar; he
was perhaps the first Italian to study Greek;
he was chosen to deliver the earliest course of
lectures on Dante. Chaucer was also a scholar;
he was a traveller and a man of affairs. Both
of them were conscious artists, masters of the
narrative art, treating the raw material they
found ready to their hands with the utmost
freedom, and understanding all the advan-

tages of selection, unity, compression, variety, proportion, movement, and climax. Their tales can be studied to-day as masterpieces of craftsmanship. They had the gift of story-telling, and also the knowledge how best to put that having to usury, and how to make it return the fullest revenue.

The two great writers whose names come next in chronological sequence in the history of fiction are Rabelais and Cervantes. The Frenchman and the Spaniard had a profounder philosophy of life than the Italian and the Englishman, but they lacked the sense of art, as the most careless contrast would show. The tales of Boccaccio and of Chaucer are swift and beautifully proportioned, while the stories of Rabelais and Cervantes are slow and lumbering. The involute clumsiness of 'Don Quixote,' considered merely as a specimen of narrative art, is indisputable; and the slovenliness of its structure, the negligence of the narrator, and his insufficient respect for the masterpiece which he had begotten unawares, are equally evident. But careless as is the scheme of 'Don Quixote,' it is superior to the wilful and sprawling formlessness of the chronicle of 'Gargantua.' The gift of story-telling, the sheer ability to hold the reader's attention by a string of adventures, put together almost at hap-hazard, and told almost as artlessly—this both Rabelais and Cervantes must needs have had.

There is no necessity now to attempt an analysis of this gift and a declaration of its constituent elements, even if it were possible to do so—which may be doubted. What is obvious enough is that it is sometimes accompanied by the keenest understanding of the principles of narrative art, and sometimes it is not so accompanied. Those who possess it may also have knowledge and wisdom, or they may not own these additional qualifications. But without some small share of this native faculty no novelist can hope to attain his purpose—no novelist, and no historian.

The author of the 'Short History of the English People' once defined the novel as "history that did not happen;" and turning this happy suggestion inside out, we may call history "fiction that did happen." Macaulay deliberately desired to write a history of England which should be read as eagerly as the latest novel, and he had his wish. Probably Green was inspired by a similar motive, and indubitably he achieved a similar triumph. The novel which Motley once wrote, and the

novel which Parkman once wrote, failed to find
favor in the eyes of the general reader, and
dropped swiftly out of sight; but yet who could
deny the gift of story-telling to the historian
of the siege of Antwerp, or to the historian of
the conspiracy of Pontiac? Prescott had the
gift also when he told the most marvellous of
all true stories, the tale of the conquest of
Mexico by Cortez and his companions. Froude
had it, even if he lacked other indispensable
qualities of the great historian ; and—to take a
long stride backward—Herodotus had it, even
though he may have availed himself now and
again of the novelist's other privileges. Xeno-
phon revealed his possession of it more in his
story of the retreat of the ten thousand, which
was fact, than in his story of the training of
Cyrus, which was fiction.

Of course it will not do to force the classification too rigorously; in art the hard and fast
lines of science are impossible. None the less
is it amusing to call the roll of English novelists, and, without insisting on an inexorable
division of the sheep from the goats, to try
and see which of them had this gift, and
which of them had to make up for a deficiency of it by an abundance in other direc-
tions. Defoe, for instance, like Le Sage, was

a story-teller above all things; he had this
precious faculty in the highest degree, and
perhaps he had little else.   Swift had it in
an equally full proportion, and he had many
other things besides; indeed, the final proof
of Swift's possession of this gift, were any
needed, might be found in the fact that owing
to it his bitter satire of his contemporaries,
his misanthropic and malignant attack on
humanity at large and for all time, survives
now as a classic of childhood, and that the
boys and girls of America in the nineteenth
century read the travels of Lemuel Gulliver
as innocently as they read the adventures of
Robinson Crusoe, with no suspicion that beneath the surface of the entrancing story there
lies an evil allegory.   This is a stroke of the
irony of fate which Swift himself would appreciate.

Of the three great English novelists of the
eighteenth century perhaps Smollett had the
most of this faculty, and Richardson the least,
although Fielding had a richer nature than
either of the others, and a finer art, and therefore he got the utmost out of his having.
Goldsmith's one attempt at fiction is engag-
ingly artless and continually interesting; Goldsmith, like Irving, who resembled him in

many other respects also, had his full share of this native faculty, though he did not cultivate it as carefully as Irving did. In like manner Cooper was a more conscientious workman than Scott, and he put his framework together better, inferior as the American romancer was to the Scottish master in richness of humor and in insight into human character.

Of the three great British novelists of the nineteenth century Dickens was the only one who was a true story-teller, having a far larger share of the native gift even than Thackeray, while George Eliot had less of it than almost any other of those who have become famous as writers of fiction. Dickens was a man of limited culture and of narrow intelligence—as his 'Pictures from Italy' proves, and his 'American Notes'—and he had absurd artistic ideals; but his was the faculty of telling a tale so that we cannot choose but hear. Thackeray, a more accomplished craftsman, was often a more careless artificer; he had a far finer intelligence than Dickens, and a deeper nature; but merely as a story-teller Dickens seems to me to be his superior.

George Eliot (like Tolstoï, another great writer who uses fiction as a medium for

morality) strikes me always as not naturally a
teller of tales, like Swift, for instance, and
Goldsmith. In reading 'Adam Bede' and
'Middlemarch,' as in reading 'Anna Karénina,'
we have a constant sense of effort, as though the
authors were struggling with a consciousness
that story-telling was not that for which they
were born. That George Eliot and Tolstoï
were not wholly devoid of the requisite endowment is evident from these books and their
fellows; but the permanent value of George
Eliot's writings and of Tolstoï's is not to be
sought in their stories considered merely as
stories. And if it were not that the 'Sorrows
of Werther' had met with instant acceptance
all over Europe, I should venture to suggest
that, great as Goethe was, his gift of story-
telling was singularly small. There is nothing
easy or spontaneous about 'Wilhelm Meister,'
as it is an effort of the intellect rather than a
story. One might call it the first *tendenz-
roman*—the first novel-with-a-purpose—if one
could make out clearly what its purpose was.
Certainly one can see in 'Wilhelm Meister'
the ancestor of 'Daniel Deronda' and of
'Robert Elsmere' and of 'John Ward, Preach-
er'—just as one can call Miss Austen the
maiden grandmother of Mr. Howells. It is

to be noted that Goethe, keen-sighted toward all things, saw himself also with clear eyes. He confessed to Eckermann that his tendency towards the practice of the plastic arts had been an error, since he had no natural disposition towards them.

(1894.)

II.—CERVANTES, ZOLA, KIPLING AND CO.

M. ANATOLE FRANCE, one of the most discriminating and inconsequent of essayists, has suggested that criticism at its best is little more than a recital of the adventures of the critic's mind in contact with masterpieces. Perhaps one reason why criticism is so infrequently at its best is that the critic's mind is in contact with masterpieces less often than it might be. It is with the writings of his contemporaries that the critic has to deal for the most part; and how few of any man's contemporaries are masters! It is only by returning resolutely again and again to the masterpieces of the past that a critic is able to sustain his standard and to prevent his taste from sinking to the level of the average of contemporary writing.

And this return, always its own reward, is not without its own surprises. Either the accepted work is worthy of its high repute— and then there is the pleasure of expounding

it afresh to a new generation and of showing
its fitness to modern conditions despite its age
—or else it is unworthy and lacks true dura-
bility—and then there is the sad duty of ex-
plaining how it deserved its fame once, and
why it is now outworn.   To one critic it happened one summer to be reading 'Don Quixote' (in Mr. Ormsby's nervous and satisfactory
translation), when he received, by the same
post, the 'Débâcle' of M. Émile Zola, and
the 'Naulahka' of Mr. Rudyard Kipling and
the late Wolcott Balestier; and when he had
made an end of the perusal of these three
books—the novel of the Spaniard, the novel
of the Frenchman, and the novel of the British
subject and the American citizen—it occurred
to him that he had in them material for a literary comparison not without a certain piquancy.
To criticise these three books adequately would
permit the writing of the history of fiction
during the past three centuries; it would au-
thorize a thorough discussion of the principles of the novelist's art, as these have been
developed by the many mighty story-tellers
who lived after Cervantes and before M. Zola.

For a siege as formidable as this I have not
the critical apparatus, even if I had the desire.
The most that I can do here is to set down

honestly and frankly a few of my impressions as I read in turn these three novels, strangely consorted and sharply contrasting. To sum up the merits of M. Zola's book is easy; and it is not hard to form and to formulate an opinion about the Indo-American tale of the two young collaborators; but the great work of Cervantes is not so lightly disposed of. The danger of any effort to record the adventures of the critic's mind in contact with a masterpiece like 'Don Quixote' is that it is exceedingly difficult for the critic to be frank with himself or honest with his readers. His mind does not come squarely in contact with the masterpiece; it is warded off by the cloud of commentators with whom every masterpiece is encompassed about. He can read only through the spectacles of the countless critics who have preceded him. He knows what he ought to think about 'Don Quixote,' and this makes it almost impossible for him to think for himself as he ought.

For the critic in search of mental adventures, it is a safeguard to have a hearty distrust of philosophic criticism, so-called—to have a profound disbelief in the allegorical interpretation of simple stories. Cervantes was like all the other great makers of fiction in that he wrote first to amuse himself and to relieve himself, and only secondarily to amuse his readers, to move them, to instruct them even.

"There is no mighty purpose in this book," is a proper motto for the title-page of most of the masterpieces in which philosophical criticism sees a myriad of mighty purposes, and which were written easily and carelessly and with no intention of creating a masterpiece, and with scarcely a thought of the message which the world has since deciphered between the lines. "He builded better than he knew" is true of most great writers; perhaps it is not wholly true of Dante and of Milton, who were conscious artists always, and careful; but it is absolutely true of Shakespeare and of Cervantes. In their pages we find many a moral which would surprise them; and into their words we are forever reading meanings of our own of which they had never a suspicion. That 'Hamlet' and 'Don Quixote' yield up to us to-day meanings and morals their straightforward authors never intended, is perhaps the best possible evidence that 'Hamlet' and 'Don Quixote' are masterpieces. The work of art which has only the meaning and the moral its maker intended, is likely to be thin and barren.

The author of ' Hamlet' was like his close contemporary, the author of ' Don Quixote,' in that he thought less apparently of the great work which has survived in the affections of the world for two centuries and a half than he thought of his other writings, now recalled chiefly because they are due to the pen which gave us also the masterpieces. Obviously, Cervantes did not read the proof of ' Don Quixote,' the first editions of which abound in printer's errors almost as many and as serious as those which mar the first folio of Shakespeare. It would be easy to maintain the assertion that Cervantes set as little store by ' Don Quixote ' as Shakespeare did by ' Hamlet ' and its fellows, the great Spaniard esteeming more highly his plays and his poems, just as Shakespeare seems to have cherished rather his poetry than his plays, each man holding lightly that which he had wrought most readily and with least effort.

Indeed, the carelessness with which Cervantes has treated his masterpiece is one of the first things to strike a critic who reads the seventeenth-century story with nineteenth-century fastidiousness. Conscious of the temerity of my opinion, and aware of the awful fate which may befall me for declaring it, I venture to suggest that the art of fiction is a finer art to-day than it was when 'Don Quixote' was written. In the whole history of story-telling there is no greater name than the name of Cervantes; but it would be a painful reflection on progress if the efforts of successive generations of novelists—however inferior to him any one of these might be—had not put the art forward. The writers of fiction nowadays are scrupulous where Cervantes was reckless; they take thought where he gave none. Merely in the mechanism of plot, in the joinery of incident, in the craftsmanship of story-telling, 'Don Quixote' is indisputably less skilful than M. Zola's 'Débâcle,' or the Kipling-Balestier 'Naulahka'—however inferior these may be in more vital points.

Consider for a moment the awkward pretence of a translation from the manuscript of the Moor, Hamet Benengeli, as needless as it is ill-sustained. Consider the frank artlessness of the narrative, with its irrelevant tales injected into the manuscript merely because Cervantes happened to have them on hand. Consider the many anachronisms and inconsistencies which Cervantes troubled himself about quite as little as Shakespeare thought or cared whether or not Bohemia was a desert

country by the sea. Consider the extraordinary series of coincidences which brought together at the inn four marvellously beautiful
women, when the captive met his brother and
Cardenio recovered Luscinda, all of which is
improbable to the vanishing-point, and all of
which, worse yet, has nothing whatever to do
with the true subject of the story. Considering all these slovenlinesses, it is impossible not
to wonder whether the art of fiction did not
retrograde with Cervantes, for both Boccaccio
and Chaucer had attained vigor and supple-
ness in narrative; their tales were naïf, no
doubt, and direct, but they were always artfully composed and presented. To this day
the ' Decameron ' and the ' Canterbury Tales '
are models of simple story-telling. Great as
are his other qualities, Cervantes, merely as a
teller of tales, is as inferior to Boccaccio and to
Chaucer as he is superior to Rabelais.

It is in its humanity, in its presentation of
men and women, in its character - drawing, as
the modern phrase is, that the story of Cervantes excels all the stories of Boccaccio, of
Chaucer, and of Rabelais. Alongside the gigantic figure of the Knight of La Mancha,
what are the characters in the brilliant little
comedies of Chaucer and of Boccaccio but

thumb-nail sketches? What are Gargantua and Panurge but broad caricatures when compared with the delicately limned Don Quixote? Where, before, had any one put into fiction so much of our everyday humanity? And what, after all, do we seek in a novel, if it is not human nature? To catch mankind in the act, as it were; to surprise the secrets of character and to show its springs; to get into literature the very trick of life itself; to display the variety of human existence, its richness, its breadth, its intensity; to do these things with unforced humor, with unfailing good-humor, with good-will towards all men, with tolerance, with benignity, with loving kindness—this is what no writer of fiction had done before Cervantes wrote 'Don Quixote,' and this is what no writer of fiction has ever done better than Cervantes did it when he wrote 'Don Quixote.'

Chaucer is shrewd and kindly at once, but even he lacks the commingled benevolence and worldly wisdom of Cervantes. The characters of the 'Canterbury Tales' have a sharper outline than the more softly rounded figures with whom Don Quixote is associated. Chaucer had a full share of the milk of human kindness, but there is the very cream of it in Cervantes.　Perhaps there is no better test of the greatness of a humorist than this—that his humor has no curdling acidity.　It is easy to amuse when there is a willingness to wound wantonly ; and Swift, though he may laugh and shake in Rabelais' easy-chair, does not fill that huge throne, because he has the pettiness of brutality.　'Gulliver' is inferior to 'Gargantua' in that the author of the former hated humanity, while the author of the latter loved his fellow-man, and took life easily and was happy.

Cervantes was not a merry man, and he had a hard life, and perhaps he wrote his great book in prison ; but there is no discontent in 'Don Quixote.'　There is a wholesome philosophy in it and a willingness to make the best of the world, a world which is not so bad, after all.　'Don Quixote' is a very long book, not so long as 'Amadis of Gaul,' or as the romances of Mademoiselle de Scudéry, or as the 'Three Musketeers' with its tail of sequels, but longer even than 'Daniel Deronda' and than 'Robert Elsmere'; it is very long and it is crowded with characters, but among all these people there is no one man or woman whom the reader hates ; there is no one whom the author despises or insults.　Cervantes is not severe with the children of his brain; he loves them all; he treats them all with the toleration which comes of perfect understanding. Here, indeed, is the quality in which he is most modern, in which he is still unsurpassable. Fielding caught it from him; and Thackeray, who borrowed so many things from Fielding and so much, did not take over this also, or he could never have pursued and run down and harried Becky Sharp as he thought fit to do.

Just as Fielding began 'Joseph Andrews' merely to guy Richardson's virtuous 'Pamela,' and just as he ended by falling in love with his own handiwork and by giving us the exquisite portrait of Parson Adams, so Cervantes, intending at first little more than to break a lance with the knights of romance, came to respect his own work more and more, and to treat Don Quixote with increasing courtesy. Much of the first part is horse-play, fun of the most robust sort. The humor of physical misadventure is rarely refined, and it takes a stout stomach to relish some of Don Quixote's earlier misfortunes. Even in the second part, the practical joke of the belled cats may fairly be called cruel, and it is altogether unworthy of the hero. Perhaps this is nineteenth-cen-

tury hypercriticism, but Cervantes is to blame
if he has presented to us a character so lovable
that we revolt when any one takes an unfair
advantage of Don Quixote.

We do not resent the indignities which befall Sancho, for he has a tough hide and a
stout heart and a mouth full of proverbs for
his own consolation. Yet, in his way, the
worthy squire is as lovable as the honorable
knight he served. Just as Sam Weller (who
made the success of the ' Pickwick Papers ')
was an afterthought, so was Sancho, who owed
his being apparently to the chance remark of
the Landlord, that a knight should be attended
by a squire. Nothing reveals the genius of
Cervantes more plainly than the development
of Sancho Panza, who was at first only a clown,
nothing but a droll, a variant of the gracioso
or low comedian accompanying the hero of
every Spanish comedy. By degrees he is ele-
vated from a mere mask into an actual man,
the mouthpiece of our common humanity.
The lofty Knight of La Mancha, with his impossible aspirations, may be taken as a personification of the soul, while Sancho is the body
—of the earth, earthy, and having his feet on
the ground firmly. " There is a moral in ' Don
Quixote,' " said Lowell, " and a very profound

one, whether Cervantes consciously put it there or not, and it is this: That whoever quarrels with the nature of things, wittingly or unwittingly, is certain to get the worst of it." Sancho had never a quarrel with the nature of things.

Lowell also reminded us that " Cervantes is the father of the modern novel, in so far as it has become a study and delineation of character, instead of being a narrative seeking to interest by situation and incident." 'Don Quixote' is one of the most original of stories; it had no predecessors of its kind, and it evolved itself by the spontaneous generation of genius. But its posterity is as ample as its ancestry was meagre. When we see Fielding's Parson Adams, or Goldsmith's Dr. Primrose, or Scott's Antiquary, we see children of Don Quixote. When we follow Mr. Pickwick in his foolish wanderings, when we listen to Tartarin of Tarascon telling of the lions he has slain, when we hear Col. Carter of Cartersville urging the desire of the Garden Spot of Virginia for an outlet to the sea, we have before us the progeny of the Knight of the Sorrowful Countenance. The make-believe of Tom Sawyer in trying to get Jim out of prison in full accordance with the authorities recalls

Don Quixote's going mad in imitation of Or-
lando ; and in the pages of an earlier American humorist than Mark Twain, in Irving's
' Knickerbocker,' there is more than a hint of
the manner of Cervantes. As Lowell puts it
sharply, "the pedigrees of books are as interesting and instructive as those of men."

If Cervantes was the father of the modern
novel, we may wonder what he would think
of some of his great-great-grandchildren.
What, for example, would be his opinion of
the ' Naulahka,' written by a Londoner who
had been East and by a New-Yorker who had
been West. Cervantes grew to manhood with
the sons of the Conquistadores, with the men
of iron who had won for Spain the golden
lands of Mexico and Peru ; would he have
foregathered with the Argonauts of Forty-
nine ? A scant half-century before his birth
the Portuguese had pushed their way around
Africa in search of Golconda and Cathay ;
would he have been interested by this story of
the West and the East ?

Of one thing, indeed, we may fairly be certain—that Cervantes would not have been at
all surprised by the manner of the ' Naulahka,'
for it is a tale of a kind he was abundantly
familiar with. It is a story of a sort older by

far than 'Don Quixote'; it is a story, in fact, of the sort that 'Don Quixote' was written to satirize. In the new tale we have new dresses, of course, and new scenery and new properties, but the tale itself is the old, old story of the hero in search of adventures; it is the tale of the hero always on the brink of death, but bearing a charmed life; it is the tale of the hero skilled in all manner of sports, expert with all manner of weapons, fertile in resource and prompt in decision; it is the tale, in short, of the bravura hero of concert-pitch romance. What is Tarvin of Topaz but Amadis of Gaul? What is the Crichton of Colorado but Palmerin of England, with all the modern improvements? What is he but Belianis of Greece brought down to date?

The death-dealing and unkillable Tarvin may also be called a Yankee D'Artagnan. Like the Gascon hero, he goes in search of jewels of great price; but he is a nobler hero even than Dumas's, for he is alone, while the three musketeers were always four. Tarvin, indeed, is the very acme of heroes, than which there can be no man more accomplished and ver-satile — not even Mr. Barnes of New York, or Mr. Potter of Texas. He is a real-estate boomer and an engineer; he has been a broncho-breaker and a telegraph operator; he is a dead shot with a revolver, hitting a half-dollar spun in the air while keeping an easy seat on a bucking horse.

The main adventure in which the heroic Tarvin is engaged is simply childish; the word need not be taken as a reproach — I merely mean that it is a thing to be told to amuse children. It is what the French call a *conte à dormir debout*. Like most of the romantic fiction of this late day, the 'Naulahka' reveals rather invention than imagination. It is ingeniously constructed; it has not a little of the cleverness its authors have shown in other work; it has passages of beauty; it gives the reader moments of excitement; it is lighted now and again by flashes of insight; and, as a whole, it is a hollow disappointment.

And the reason is not far to seek. It is because romance of this sort is not what either of the collaborators did best. It is because neither Mr. Kipling nor his brother-in-law could put his whole strength into so hopeless a make-believe. Balestier was a realist; beyond all question, the man who wrote the little tale of 'Reffey' was a realist, with the imagination a true realist needs more than the ordinary romanticist.   Mr. Kipling is sometimes a realist and sometimes an idealist; he is a humorist often, and, when he is at his best, he is a poet also.   Why did two such men join forces in a vain effort to pump the breath of life into a disestablished idol?

Of course, the 'Naulahka' is not without touches of character worthy of the author of the 'Courting of Dinah Shadd,' although there is little or nothing in it really worthy of the author of the 'Gate of a Hundred Sorrows' and of 'Without Benefit of Clergy.' The gypsy queen is a fine conception, and her son is a live child, and the heir-apparent is also a human being; all of these ring true. And here and there in the Indian chapters of the story are other evidences of Mr. Kipling's robust talent, of his knack of the unhackneyed epithet, of his power of revealing character as by a lightning flash.   Perhaps it is due to the milder influence of his collaborator that there is in the 'Naulahka' less of the bluster, of the swagger, of the precocious knowingness which made some of the 'Plain Tales from the Hills' offensive in the eyes of those who do not like a style made up wholly of the primary colors. There is less also of the violence which was the key-note of the 'Light that Failed'; and

12

Mr. Kipling is no longer looking for effects, immediate, obvious, and barbaric—like the architecture of the India his stories give us so strong a desire not to visit.

While the 'Naulahka' is, as I have said, the kind of a story which was popular a full century before 'Don Quixote' was written, 'La Débâcle' is the kind of a story which has come into fashion two and a half centuries after 'Don Quixote' first appeared. If Cervantes would find himself at home in reading the adventures of Tarvin of Topaz, what would he think of M. Zola's solidly built and broadly painted panorama of the Second Empire's catastrophe? Perhaps, as an old soldier, as one who had fought at Lepanto, Cervantes would be most impressed by the sustained force of M. Zola's battle-pieces, than which there are none more vigorous in all fiction. Not Stendhal's Waterloo, not Victor Hugo's, not Thackeray's—done by indirection, but all the more moving for that — not Tolstoï's Sebastopol even, gives the reader so vivid a realization of the waste of war, of its destructiveness, of the weariness of it and the hunger, of the horrors of every kind which are inevitable and necessary, and which M. Zola makes us feel more keenly than Callot could or Verestchagin.

There is in 'La Débâcle' little of the realism
M. Zola has praised, little or nothing of the
naturalism he has proclaimed; there is an
epic simplicity, a mighty movement, a cyclo-
pean architecture not to be found in the
work of any other novelist in all the luminous
list of names since Cervantes.   We have here
no miniature portraits of dandy soldiers; we
have no mere genre - painting of troops in
picturesque attitudes; we have rather a series
of masterly frescoes, brushed in boldly with
a broad sweep of the arm, without hesitancy,
with the consciousness of strength.   M. Zola
has Taine's faculty of accumulating typical
details; he has the same power of handling
immense masses of facts and of compelling
each into its proper place; and never has he
used this faculty and this power to better
advantage than in 'La Débâcle'—not even in
'Germinal.'

The story is far too long; it has two hundred pages too many; it is extended to include
the last wild struggle of the Commune; it
grows wearisome at last; but what a splendid
succession of pictures is presented to us before
we feel the first fatigue!   We are made to see
the incredible mismanagement of the imperial
army, due to mingled knavery and incompe-

tence; we are shown the complete collapse of the French commissariat and ordnance department; we are made spectators of the moral disintegration of impending defeat as the French were shut in by the inexorable iron ring of the Germans; we have brought before us the whole helpless empire, from the invalid monarch down to the privates and the peasants.

The unending passage of the Prussian artillery through the village by night at a hard gallop; the sudden vision, in the midst of the battle, of a peasant ploughing peacefully, in a hidden hollow—repeated again when the fight is over; the execution of Weiss under the eyes of his wife, after a defence of his house, which is a realization in words of the 'Last Cartridge'; the ghastly group of the dead Zouaves carousing; the frantic charge of the riderless horses across the silent battle-field; the assassination of Goliath in the presence of his child; these are things which cling to the memory obstinately. These are scenes also which Cervantes would appreciate as he would appreciate the massive structure of 'La Débâcle' when compared with the haphazard incidents and the hesitating plot of 'Don Quixote.'

What Cervantes would most miss in M. Zola's book would be joyousness and humor.

M. Zola has no humor, either positive or negative — positive which breaks in upon the
seriousness of the reader, or negative which
prevents the author from taking himself too
seriously. M. Zola has little joy in life, although
he has softened of late.   Once he saw all mankind darkly, as though he hated humanity or
despised it; and the characters in his novels
were etched by the acid of his malice.   Now
he uses a gentler crayon and he sketches with
suaver outlines; he is not unfair even towards
the Germans. There are in 'La Débâcle'
men and women we can like—although there
is no one to love as we love Don Quixote and
Sancho.   Brutal is what M. Zola used to be,
brutal and dirty. He is not brutal now and
he is less dirty. He is still fond of foul words,
and there are half a dozen of them repeated
again and again in 'La Débâcle.'   But as a
whole, the story is surprisingly clean.   There
is nothing in it to shock Cervantes certainly,
for he too could be plain-spoken at times—
quite as plain-spoken as M. Zola.   But whatever his speech, however frank and hearty,
however exactly he reproduces the vocabulary
of the common people, the mind of Cervantes
was always clean, pure, lofty.

(1892.)

III.—THE PROSE TALES OF M. FRANÇOIS COPPÉE.

LIKE Molière, like Boileau, like Regnard, like Voltaire, and like Musset, M. François Coppée was born in Paris, and more than any other of the half-dozen is he a true child of the fair city by the Seine, loving her more ardently, and leaving her less willingly. The facts of his simple and uneventful career have been set forth by his friend M. de Lescure in 'François Coppée: l'Homme, la Vie et l'Œuvre (1842–1889).' From this we learn that the poet was born in 1842, that he was the youngest child of a poor clerk in the War Department, that he had three elder sisters, one of whom survives still to take care of her brother, that he spent most of his struggling childhood in old houses on the left (and more literary) bank of the Seine, that he was not an apt scholar in his youth, that he began to write verses very early in his teens, and that at last his father died, and he succeeded to the modest position in the War Department, becoming the head of the family at twenty-one. In time he made acquaintance with other young poets, and was admitted into the " Parnassians," as they were called —followers of Victor Hugo, of Théophile Gautier, of Théodore de Banville, students of new and old rhythms, and seekers after rich rymes, as ardent in the search as the Argonauts of ' Forty-nine. M. Coppée burned every one of his juvenile poems, and wrote many another of more cunning workmanship; and of these newer poems two volumes were published in the next few years—' Le Réliquaire' and 'Les Intimités'—but they did not sell two hundred copies all told.

Then, in 1869, came the first golden gleam of fortune. ' Le Passant,' a little one-act comedy in verse, was acted one night at the Odéon, and the next day the name of François Coppée was no longer unknown to any of those who care for letters. 'Le Passant' is undeniably artificial, and at bottom it is probably forced in feeling, if not false; but beyond all question the poet believed in it and accepted its truth, and delighted in his work. The sentiment is charmingly youthful, with a springlike freshness, and the versification is absolutely impeccable. For years M. Coppée was called "the author of 'Le Passant,'" until he came almost to hate his first-born. But only one of his later plays has rivalled it in popular acceptance; this is the pathetic 'Luthier de Crémone,' of which there are several adaptations in English. A third one-act play, 'Le Pater,' forbidden in Paris by the stage censors, was, strangely enough, brought out here in New York at Daly's Theatre shortly after as the 'Prayer.' As a dramatist, M. Coppée continues the romanticist tradition, now a little outworn; and his longer plays lack the directness of his later poems and prose tales. No one of them has had more than a merely honorable success, and no one of them—with a single exception only—has shown itself strong enough to stand the perils of translation.

During the dark days of 1870 and 1871 M. Coppée did his duty in the ranks, like many another artist in letters and with the brush. Of course, he wrote war poems, both during the fighting and after, neither better nor worse, most of them, than the war poems of other French poets. Better than any of these martial rymes are the 'Grève des Forgerons,' written just before the war, and 'Les Humbles,' a volume of verse written shortly after peace had been restored. The 'Grève des Forgerons' is a dramatic monologue, in which a striking iron-worker explains how it came to pass that he killed a man, and why he did the deed. It suggests Browning in its mingling of movement and introspection, but it is neither as rugged in form nor as swift in action as the British poet would have made it.

It is in 'Les Humbles' that there was first revealed the French poet with whom we of Anglo-Saxon stock can perhaps feel ourselves most in sympathy. The note which dominates the poems in that collection, and in most of M. Coppée's later volumes of verse, is less seldom found in English literature than in French. This is the note of sympathy with the lowly, with the unsuspected victims of fate. It is the note of compassion for those who struggle secretly and in vain, for those who are borne down beneath the burdens of commonplace existence, for those who have never had a chance in life. It is the note we mark now and again, for instance, in the deeper poems of Mr. Austin Dobson. Many of the foremost French authors of late years are mere mandarins, writing exclusively for their peers; they are Brahmins, despising all outside their own high caste; they are wholly without bowels of compassion for their fellow-man. Compare, for example, again, the contemptuous and contemning attitude of Flaubert towards the creatures of his own making, whom he regards distantly, as though they were doubtful insects under a microscope, and the warmer tolerance George Eliot shows even for her least worthy characters.

M. Coppée is as detached from his humble heroes and heroines as any one could wish; he is too profoundly an artist ever to intervene in his own person; but he is not chill and inaccessible in his telling of their little lives, made up of a thousand banalities and lit by a single gleam of poetry, not cast by the glare of a great self-sacrifice, but falling from the pure flame of daily duties performed without thought of self. 'Les Humbles' is but a gallery of pictures in the manner of the little masters of Holland—a series of portraits of the down-trodden in their every-day garb, with that suggestion of their inner life which illuminates every painting by an artist of true insight. In the old-fashioned sense of the word there is little "heroic" in 'Les Humbles;' and there is absolutely nothing of the exaggerated larger-than-life-and-twice-as-natural manner of Victor Hugo, set off with violent contrasts and startling antitheses. Instead we have an accomplished poet telling us of the simple lives of the poor in the simple speech of the people. M. Coppée has a homeliness of phrase not unlike that of Theocritus, but perhaps less consciously literary.

Indeed, nothing more clearly shows the delicacy of his art than his extraordinary skill in concealing all trace of artifice, so that a most carefully constructed poem is seemingly spontaneous. To most of us French poetry is rarely interesting; it is obviously artificial; it strikes us as somewhat remote; possibly from the enforced use of words of Romance origin (which therefore seem to us secondary) to describe heartfelt emotion, expressed by us in words of Teutonic stock (which are therefore to us primary). Lowell has told us that it is only the high polish of French verse that keeps out decay. We do not feel this in reading the best of M. Coppée's poetry; it seems to us as natural an outgrowth almost as Heine's or Longfellow's. In another essay Lowell says that perhaps the great charm of Gray's 'Elegy' is to be found " in its embodying that pensively stingless pessimism which comes with the first gray hair, that vague sympathy with ourselves which is so much cheaper than sympathy with others, that placid melancholy which satisfies the general appetite for an emotion that titillates rather than wounds." That M. Coppée has put into French verse, unmusical as it is, the qualities which Lowell finds in Gray's ' Elegy ' is evidence that neither in manner nor in matter is he like most French poets.

But this acceptability of his poetry to ears attuned to more Teutonic rhythms has not been won by any accidental dereliction from the strictest rule of the Parnassians. M. Coppée has besieged and captured the final fastnesses of French metrical art, and his work is completely satisfactory even to Banville, who bestrides his hobby of "rich" rymes as though it were Pegasus itself. M. Coppée early gave proof of remarkable skill at the difficult game of French versification, and he still plays it scientifically, and with great good luck. Of late years he has been called upon frequently to sing to order, to write verses for a celebration, and he has always been as ready as Dr. Holmes was once to lay a garland of rymes on the grave of a hero. The art of writing occasional verse which shall be worthy of the occasion is not a common gift. M. Coppée possesses it abundantly, and his many poems for feasts or fasts are always appropriate, adequate, and dignified.

'Olivier' is M. Coppée's most ambitious longer poem. But it is not in his longer poems that he is seen at his best. What he does to perfection is the *conte en vers*—the tale in verse. The *conte* is a form of fiction in which the French have always delighted, and in which they have always excelled, from the days of the *jongleurs* and the *trouvères*, past the periods of La Fontaine and Voltaire, down to the present. The *conte* is a tale something more than a sketch, it may be, and something less than a short story. In verse it is at times but a mere rymed anecdote, or it may attain almost to the direct swiftness of a ballad. The 'Canterbury Tales' are *contes* most of them, if not all, and so are some of the 'Tales of a Way-side Inn.' The free-and-easy tales of Prior were written in imitation of the French *conte en vers;* and that likewise was the model of more than one of the lively narrative poems of Mr. Austin Dobson.

No one has succeeded more admirably in the *conte en vers* than M. Coppée. Where was there ever anything better of its kind than 'L'Enfant de la Balle'?—that gentle portrait of the infant phenomenon, framed in a chain of occasional gibes at the sordid ways of theatrical managers, and at their hostility toward poetic plays. Where is there anything of a more simple pathos than ' L'Épave ' ?—that story of a sailor's son whom the widowed mother vainly strives to keep from the cruel waves that killed his father. (It is worthy of a parenthesis that although the ship M. Coppée loves best is that which sails the blue shield of the city of Paris, he knows the sea also, and he depicts sailors with affectionate fidelity.) But whether at the sea-side by chance, or more often in the streets of the city, the poet seeks for the subject of his story some incident of daily occurrence made significant by his interpretation ; he chooses some character commonplace enough, but made firmer by conflict with evil and by victory over self. Those whom he puts into his poems are still the humble, the forgotten, the neglected, the unknown, and it is the feelings and the struggles of these that he tells us, with no maudlin sentimentality, and with no dead-set at our sensibilities. The sub-title Mrs. Stowe gave to ' Uncle Tom's Cabin ' would serve to cover most of M. Coppée's *contes* either in prose or verse ; they are nearly all pictures of "life among the lowly." But there is no forcing of the note in his painting of poverty

and labor; there is no harsh juxtaposition of
the blacks and the whites. The tone is always
manly and wholesome.

'La Marchande de Journaux' and the other
little masterpieces of story-telling in verse are
unfortunately untranslatable, as are all poems
but a lyric or two now and then by a happy
accident. A translated poem is a boiled straw-
berry, as some one once brutally put it. But
the tales which M. Coppée has written in prose
—a true poet's prose, nervous, vigorous, flex-
ible, and firm—these can be Englished by taking thought and time and pains, without which
a translation is always a betrayal. Ten of these
tales have been rendered into English by Mr.
Learned, and the ten chosen for translation
are among the best of the twoscore and more of
M. Coppée's *contes en prose*. These ten tales
are fairly representative of his range and variety. Compare, for example, the passion in
the 'Foster-sister'—pure, burning, and fatal—
with the Black Forest *naïveté* of the 'Wooden
Shoes of Little Wolff.' Contrast the touching
pathos of the 'Substitute,' poignant in his mag-
nificent self-sacrifice, by which the man who
has conquered his shameful past goes back
willingly to the horrible life he has fled from,
that he may save from a like degradation and

from an inevitable moral decay the one friend
he has in the world, all unworthy as this friend
is—contrast this with the story of the gigantic
deeds 'My Friend Meutrier' boasts about unceasingly, not knowing that he has been discovered in his little round of daily domestic
duties—making the coffee of his good old
mother, and taking her poodle out for a
walk.

Among these ten there are tales of all sorts,
from the tragic adventure of 'An Accident' to
the pendant portraits of the 'Two Clowns,' cut-
ting in its sarcasm, but not bitter; from the
'Captain's Vices,' which suggests at once
George Eliot's 'Silas Marner' and Mr. Austin
Dobson's 'Tale of Polypheme,' to the sombre
reverie of the poet 'At the Table,' a sudden
and searching light cast on the labor and mis-
ery which underlie the luxury of our complex
modern existence. Like 'At the Table,' the
'Dramatic Funeral' is a picture more than it
is a story; it is a marvellous reproduction of
the factitious emotion of the good-natured
stage-folk, who are prone to overact even their
own griefs and joys. The 'Dramatic Funeral'
seems to me always as though it might be a
painting of M. Jean Béraud, that most Parisian
of artists, just as certain stories of Maupas-

sant's inevitably suggest the bold freedom of M. Forain's sketches in black and white.

An ardent admirer of the author of the stories in the 'Odd Number' has protested to me that M. Coppée is not an etcher like Maupassant, but rather a painter in water-colors. And why not? Thus might we call M. Alphonse Daudet an artist in pastels, so adroitly does he suggest the very bloom of color. No doubt M. Coppée's *contes* have not the sharpness of Maupassant's nor the brilliancy of M. Daudet's. But what of it? They have qualities of their own. They have sympathy, poetry, and a power of suggesting pictures not exceeded, I think, by those of either Maupassant or M. Daudet. M. Coppée's street views in Paris, his interiors, his impressionist sketches of life under the shadow of Notre Dame, are convincingly successful. They are intensely to be enjoyed by those of us who take the same keen delight in the varied phases of life in New York. They are not, to my mind, really rivalled either by those of Maupassant, who was a Norman by birth and a nomad by choice, or by those of M. Daudet, who is a native of Provence, although now for thirty years a resident of Paris. M. Coppée is a Parisian from his youth up, and even in prose

13

he is a poet. Perhaps this is why his pictures of Paris are unsurpassable in their felicity
and in their verity.

It may be fancy, but I seem to see also a
finer morality in M. Coppée's work than in
Maupassant's, or in M. Daudet's, or in that of
almost any other of the Parisian story-tellers
of to-day. In his tales we breathe a purer
moral atmosphere, more wholesome and more
bracing. It is not that M. Coppée probably
thinks of ethics rather than esthetics; in this
respect his attitude is undoubtedly that of the
others. There is no sermon in his song, or at
least none for those who will not seek it for
themselves; there is never a hint of a preach-
ment. But for all that, I have found in his
work a trace of the tonic morality which in-
heres in Molière, for example—also a Parisian
by birth—and in Rabelais, too, despite his dis-
guising grossness. This finer morality comes
possibly from a wider and a deeper survey of
the universe; and it is as different as possible
from the morality which is externally applied,
and which always punishes the villain in the
fifth act.

It is of good augury for our own letters that
the best French fiction of to-day is getting itself translated in the United States, and that

the liking for it is growing apace. Fiction is more consciously an art in France than anywhere else, perhaps partly because the French are now foremost in nearly all forms of artistic endeavor. In the short story especially, in the tale, in the *conte*, their supremacy is incontestable, and their skill is shown and their esthetic instinct exemplified partly in the sense of form, in the constructive method which underlies the best short stories, however trifling these may appear to be, and partly in the rigorous suppression of non-essentials, due in a measure, it may be, to the example of Mérimée. That is an example we in America may study to advantage, and from the men who are writing fiction in France we may gain much.

(1890.)

IV.—THE SHORT STORIES OF M. LUDOVIC HALÉVY

To most American readers of fiction I fancy that M. Ludovic Halévy is known chiefly, if not solely, as the author of that most charming of modern French novels, the 'Abbé Constantin.' Some of these readers may have disliked this or that novel of M. Zola's because of its bad moral, and this or that novel of M. Ohnet's because of its bad taste, but all of them were delighted to discover in M. Halévy's interesting and artistic work a story written by a French gentleman for young ladies. Here and there a scoffer might sneer at the tale of the old French priest and the young women from Canada as innocuous but saccharine; but the story of the good Abbé Constantin and of his nephew, and of the girl the nephew loved in spite of her American millions—this story had the rare good fortune of pleasing at once the broad public of indiscriminate readers of fiction and the narrower circle of real lovers of literature. Artificial the atmosphere of the tale might be, but it was with an artifice at once delicate and delicious; and the tale itself won its way into the hearts of the women of America as it had into the hearts of the women of France.

There is even a legend—although how solid a foundation it may have in fact I do not dare to discuss—there is a legend that the lady-superior of a certain convent near Paris was so fascinated by the 'Abbé Constantin,' and so thoroughly convinced of the piety of its author, that she ordered all his other works, receiving in due season the lively volumes wherein are recorded the sayings and doings of Monsieur and Madame Cardinal, and of the two lovely daughters of Monsieur and Madame Cardinal. To note that these very amusing studies of certain aspects of life in a modern capital originally appeared in that extraordinary journal *La Vie Parisienne*—now sadly degenerate—is enough to indicate that they are not precisely what the good lady-superior expected to receive. We may not say that the 'Famille Cardinal' is one of the books every gentleman's library should be without; but to appreciate its value requires a far different knowledge of the world and of

its wickedness than is needed to understand
the 'Abbé Constantin.'

Yet the picture of the good priest and the
portraits of the little Cardinals are the work
of the same hand, plainly enough. In both
of these books, as in 'Criquette' (M. Halévy's
only other novel), as in 'A Marriage for Love'
and the two-score other short stories he has
written during the past thirty years, there are
the same artistic qualities, the same sharpness
of vision, the same gentle irony, the same constructive skill, and the same dramatic touch.
It is to be remembered always that the author
of the 'Abbe Constantin' is also the half-
author of 'Froufrou' and of 'Tricoche et Cacolet,' as well as of the librettos of the 'Belle
Hélène' and of the 'Grande Duchesse de
Gerolstein.'

In the two novels, as in the two-score short
stories and sketches—the *contes* and the *nou-
velles* which are now spring-like idyls and now
wintry episodes, now sombre etching and now
gayly colored pastels—in all the works of the
story-teller we see the firm grasp of the dramatist. The characters speak for themselves;
each reveals himself with the swift directness
of the personages of a play. They are not
talked about and about, for all analysis has

been done by the playwright before he rings up the curtain in the first paragraph. And the story unrolls itself, also, as rapidly as does a comedy. The movement is straightforward. There is the cleverness and the ingenuity of the accomplished dramatist, but the construction has the simplicity of the highest skill. The arrangement of incidents is so artistic that it seems inevitable; and no one is ever moved to wonder whether or not the tale might have been better told in different fashion.

Nephew of the composer of 'La Juive'—an opera not now heard as often as it deserves, perhaps—and son of a playwright no one of whose productions now survives, M. Halévy grew up in the theatre. At fourteen he was on the free-list of the Opéra, the Opéra Comique, and the Odéon. After he left school and went into the civil service his one wish was to write plays, and so to be able to afford to resign his post. In the civil service he had an inside view of French politics, which gave him a distaste for the mere game of government without in any way impairing the vigor of his patriotism—as is proved by certain of the short stories dealing with the war of 1870 and the revolt of the Paris Communists. And while he did his work faithfully, he had spare hours to give to literature. He wrote plays and stories, and they were rejected. The manager of the Odéon declared that one early play of M. Halévy's was exactly suited to the Gymnase, and the manager of the Gymnase protested that it was exactly suited to the Odéon. The editor of a daily journal said that one early tale of M. Halévy's was too brief for a novel, and the editor of a weekly paper said that it was too long for a short story.

In time, of course, his luck turned; he had plays performed and stories published; and at last he met M. Henri Meilhac, and entered on that collaboration of nearly twenty years' duration to which we owe 'Froufrou' and 'Tricoche et Cacolet' on the one hand, and on the other the books of Offenbach's most brilliant operas—'Barbebleue,' for example, and 'La Périchole.' When this collaboration terminated, shortly before M. Halévy wrote the 'Abbé Constantin,' he gave up writing for the stage. The training of the playwright he could not give up, if he would, nor the intimacy with the manners and customs of the people who live, move, and have their being on the far side of the curtain.

Obviously M. Halévy is fond of the actors

and the actresses with whom he spent the years of his manhood. They appear again and again in his tales; and in his treatment of them there is never anything ungentlemanly, as there was in M. Jean Richepin's volume of theatrical sketches. M. Halévy's liking for the men and women of the stage is deep; and wide is his knowledge of their changing moods. The young Criquette and the old Karikari and the aged Dancing-master — he knows them all thoroughly, and he likes them heartily, and he sympathizes with them cordially. Indeed, nowhere can one find more kindly portraits of the kindly player-folk than in the writings of this half-author of 'Froufrou'; it is as though the successful dramatist felt ever grateful towards the partners of his toil, the companions of his struggles. He is not blind to their manifold weaknesses, nor is he the dupe of their easy emotionalism, but he is tolerant of their failings, and towards them, at least, his irony is never mordant.

Irony is one of M. Halévy's chief characteristics, perhaps the chiefest. It is gentle when he deals with the people of the stage — far gentler then than when he is dealing with the people of society, with fashionable folk, with the aristocracy of wealth. When he is telling

us of the young loves of millionaires and of
million-heiresses, his touch may seem caressing,
but for all its softness the velvet paw has claws
none the less. It is amusing to note how often
M. Halévy has chosen to tell the tale of love
among the very rich. The heroine of the
'Abbé Constantin' is immensely wealthy, as
we all know, and immensely wealthy are the
heroines of 'Princesse,' of 'A Grand Marriage,'
and of 'In the Express.' Sometimes the heroes
and the heroines are not only immensely
wealthy, they are also of the loftiest birth;
such, for instance, are the young couple whose
acquaintance we make in 'Only a Waltz.'

There is no trace or taint of snobbery in M.
Halévy's treatment of all this magnificence;
there is none of the vulgarity which marks the
pages of 'Lothair,' for example; there is no
mean admiration of mean things. There is,
on the other hand, no bitterness of scourging
satire. He lets us see that all this luxury is a
little cloying, and perhaps not a little enervating. He suggests (although he takes care never
to say it) that perhaps wealth and birth are not
really the best the world can offer. The amiable egotism of the hero of 'In the Express,'
and the not unkindly selfishness of the heroine
of that most Parisian love-story, are set before

us without insistence, it is true, but with an irony so keen that even he who runs as he reads may not mistake the author's real opinion of the characters he has evoked.

To say this is to say that M. Halévy's irony is delicate and playful. There is no harshness in his manner and no hatred in his mind. We do not find in his pages any of the pessimism which is perhaps the dominant characteristic of the best French fiction of our time. To M. Halévy, as to every thinking man, life is serious, no doubt, but it need not be taken sadly, or even solemnly. To him life seems still enjoyable, as it must to most of those who have a vivid sense of humor. He is not disillusioned utterly, he is not reduced to the blankness of despair as are so many of the disciples of Flaubert, who are cast into the outer darkness, and who hopelessly revolt against the doom they have brought on themselves.

Indeed, it is Mérimée that M. Halévy would hail as his master, and not Flaubert, whom most of his fellow French writers of fiction follow blindly. Now, while the author of 'Sâlammbo' was a romanticist turned sour, the author of 'Carmen' was a sentimentalist sheathed in irony. To Gustave Flaubert the world was hideously ugly, and he wished it strangely and splendidly beautiful, and he detested it the more because of his impossible ideal. To Prosper Mérimée the world was what it is, to be taken and made the best of, every man keeping himself carefully guarded. Like Mérimée, M. Halévy is detached, but he is not disenchanted. His work is more joyous than Mérimée's, if not so vigorous and compact, and his delight in it is less disguised. Even in the Cardinal sketches there is nothing that leaves an acrid after-taste, nothing corroding — as there is not seldom in the stronger and sterner short stories of Maupassant.

More than Maupassant or Flaubert or Mérimée is M. Halévy a Parisian. Whether or not the characters of his tale are dwellers in the capital, whether or not the scene of his story is laid in the city by the Seine, the point of view is always Parisian. The Circus Charger did his duty in the stately avenues of a noble country place, and Blacky performed his task near a rustic waterfall; but the men who record their intelligent actions are Parisians of the strictest sect. Even in the patriotic pieces called forth by the war of 1870, in the ' Insurgent ' and in the ' Chinese Ambassador,' it is the siege of Paris and the struggle of the Communists which seem to the author most important. His style even, his swift and limpid prose—the prose which somehow corresponds to the best *vers de société* in its brilliancy and buoyancy—is the style of one who lives at the centre of things. Cardinal Newman once said that while Livy and Tacitus and Terence and Seneca wrote Latin, Cicero wrote Roman; so while M. Zola on the one side, and M. Georges Ohnet on the other, may write French, M. Halévy writes Parisian.

(1893.)

V.—MR. CHARLES DUDLEY WARNER AS A WRITER OF FICTION

THE late Matthew Arnold had a far wider outlook than any of his contemporaries among British critics, but none the less was he capable of insularity on occasion, as when he made his taunting remark about the people of the United States reading the works of "a native author named Roe" rather than the masterpieces of literature—the remark being made at the very moment when the people of Great Britain were reading the works of a native author named Haggard, when the people of France were reading the works of a native author named Ohnet, and when the people of Germany were reading the works of a native author named "Marlitt." And yet a few years before the distinguished critic sneered thus inexpensively at this transient failing of ours, which happened to have at the time an equivalent in every other country, there was another American weakness at which he could have girded more effectively. This weakness was an uneasy desire for a strange and portentous work of fiction which was to be hailed at once, on its appearance, as The Great American Novel. The satirist would have had a fair target in this parochial expectancy of the impossible. How should there ever be so monstrous an entity as The Great American Novel? Is there such a thing as The Great British Novel, or The Great French Novel? And if there is, what is the name thereof, and who proclaimed and proved its unique greatness?

It is pleasant to observe that this silly demand for an impossible object, frequent enough when we had no novelists, or very few, has died away now that we have a compact corps of trained writers of fiction — a corps in which promising recruits are enlisted almost every month. These conscripts in story-telling are often veterans in other divisions of the literary body; and they are drawn especially from the rapidly thinning ranks of the essayists. It may be doubted whether the historians of literature have hitherto paid sufficient attention to the strong influence of the English essayists upon the development of the English novel. Addison and Steele made the way straight for Henry Fielding and for Jane Austen. 'Rasselas' and the 'Vicar of Wakefield' are simply numbers of the *Rambler* and of the *Citizen of the World* somewhat expanded. So Curtis, after the 'Potiphar Papers,' wrote 'Prue and I' and 'Trumps'; so Mr. Howells, after 'Suburban Sketches,' set out on 'Their Wedding Journey' and formed 'A Chance Acquaintance'; so Mr. Charles Dudley Warner, after spending a 'Summer in a Garden,' and after making a series of 'Back-Log Studies,' went away also on 'Their Pilgrimage,' and took part in 'A Little Journey in the World.'

It was Moore who pointed out in his memoir of Sheridan that English comedy had been the work of very young men—which would tend to account for its vivacity, perhaps, and for its immaturity also. That the novelists of our language have, on the contrary, flowered later in life, more often than not, has also been noted before now. Richardson was fifty when he celebrated the triumph of virtue in 'Pamela'; Fielding was thirty-five when he made fun of poor Pamela by giving her a brother, 'Joseph Andrews'; Scott was forty when he finally finished

' Waverley '; Thackeray did not begin ' Vanity Fair,' and George Eliot did not sketch the first of her ' Scenes of Clerical Life,' until they had reached one-half of the allotted limit of threescore years and ten ; and Mr. Howells was about the same age when he took his first timid flight in fiction with ' Their Wedding Journey.' Mr. Warner was older than Richardson when he turned story-teller and wrote the fascinating journal of ' Their Pilgrimage,' and he was full sixty when he followed this travel tale with a full-fledged novel, 'A Little Journey in the World.' Like Fielding and Scott, like Thackeray and Mr. Howells, Mr. Warner had made proof of his literary faculty long before he ventured into the doubtful labyrinth of fiction, wherein the most accomplished man of letters may lose his way if he cannot keep a firm grasp of the thread of interest, the only clew which can guide him and his readers to a joyful safety.

It is characteristic of Mr. Warner's modesty that even now, when he has come to his reward, when he has made a hit as a humorist, when he has been welcomed as a writer of travels, when he has won a place for himself in the front rank of essayists, when he has appeared thrice as a novelist, that he is wont

14

to speak of himself not as a man of letters, but as a journalist. His career has the unexpectedness to be discovered in the lives of so many energetic Americans who set out in one direction and then go suddenly in another— reaching their original goal in the end, it may be, but only after a circumnavigation of the globe. Born in Massachusetts in 1829, graduating from Hamilton in 1851, he lived on the frontier for a year or two, and then studied law at the University of Pennsylvania — although I must confess that the critic who sits in the Editor's Study does not look in the least like the " Philadelphia lawyer " of popular fancy. He practised law in Chicago until 1860, when he went to Hartford to take charge of a paper since consolidated with the *Courant* (in which Mr. Warner is still interested).

It was in the spring of 1870 that Mr. Warner began to contribute to the *Courant* a series of papers chronicling the experiences and the misadventures of an amateur gardener. Amusing as these little essays were, they had none of the " acrobatic comedy" (as it has been called) of the ordinary newspaper funny man, who has his easily learned formulas for extracting laughs. The humor of Mr. Warner's record of his tribulations in the garden was not machine-made ; it was original, individual, delicate, playful, and at bottom thoughtful ; it was the easy fooling of a gentleman and a scholar. It happened to hit the popular taste, and the successive papers were copied far and wide, and quoted and talked about, and finally gathered into a book, for which Henry Ward Beecher wrote a preface — omitted from the later editions now that Mr. Warner has ceased to need an introduction. ' My Summer in a Garden ' was popular not only in the United States but in Great Britain as well, where, indeed, three rival publishers showed their appreciation by reprinting it promptly. One of these gentry even changed the title and chose to call the little book ' Pusley '; but no one of the three thought it needful to transmit any pecuniary honorarium to the American author, in spite of the fact that it was even then possible to make transfers of money by the Atlantic cable.

After the success of ' My Summer in a Garden,' the author bound up in a book a selection of ' Saunterings,' an apt title for sketches of travel. Then he wrote a series of ' Back-Log Studies,' suggested possibly by the ' Autocrat of the Breakfast Table,' and possibly by the ' Reveries of a Bachelor,' and

possibly owing nothing to either of these, for
it was full of what we now know to be the
flavor of Mr. Warner's own personality. The
first requisite of an essayist, the one thing
needful, without which he is as nothing, is to
have his own point of view, to own himself,
to be his own master. The artist, so Goethe
tells us, "make what contortions he will, can
bring to light only his own individuality";
Mr. Warner is no literary contortionist, and
it is without violence or wrench that he brings
his individuality to light. The more amusing
side of this individuality had been shown in
'My Summer in a Garden,' and it was rather
the deeper aspect which was first revealed in
'Back-Log Studies,' wherein the wit and the
humor flame up and crackle and sparkle,
while the thought beneath glows and burns
steadily.

Probably Mr. Warner himself would not ap-
prove of any suggestion that all his various writings, his editorial articles, his essays, his books
of travels, his biographies, his social studies—
or at least such of them as had appeared before 1886—were merely preparations for their
author's first venture into fiction. But certainly, and whatever their value may be in
other respects, they were each in its different

degree advantageous to him when he took up
the new art of story-telling. In writing them
Mr. Warner had trained his eye and his hand ;
he had proved his weapons, and he had meas-
ured himself. The change of the essayist into
the novelist was a slow development, and not
a sudden expansion, as had been the change
of the lawyer into the journalist a quarter of
a century before. He could not but be aware
that he had the literary faculty in a high degree; it remained to be seen whether he had
also the gift of story-telling, without which
the novelist is as naught.

It does not seem to me that this crucial
question is answered in 'Their Pilgrimage.'
In this first attempt Mr. Warner was diffident
and modest. While there is more incident in
'Their Pilgrimage' than there was in Curtis's
first attempt at fiction, the 'Potiphar Papers,'
and more even than there is in Mr. Howells's
'Their Wedding Journey,' still the book is
hardly to be classed among novels, unless, indeed, there were a separate division for topo-
graphic fiction. It is the record of a voyage
of discovery among the American summer
resorts, extending from Bar Harbor to the
White Sulphur, and including Saratoga and
Long Branch, Newport and Narragansett Pier

and Niagara. It was natural that the essayist turning novelist should be a portrayer of social conditions rather than a story-teller, pure and simple. He has a story to tell, of course (he is no needy knife-grinder), and he tells it well, bringing the hero to the proposal promptly, and allowing the heroine the cherished privilege of self-sacrifice ; but none the less are we allowed to guess that the shifting panorama is almost as interesting as are the figures making love in the foreground. Now and again, as is the duty of the essayist, he lets us catch a glimpse of his own individuality, not suppressing it vigorously, as is the wont of the most advanced story-tellers of to-day.

But still, the book " lets itself be read," to use the useful German phrase. However slight as a story, it is delightful as the work of an accomplished man of letters, deftly sketching a bit of scenery here and adroitly outlining a bit of character there. And especially does it abound in good talk—in good talk which is not merely a sequence of clever phrases, but really *talk*, with the flavor of give and take, to and fro, hit or miss, cut and thrust, which is the essence of friendly conversation. The late Lord Houghton declared that " good conversation is to ordinary talk what whist is

to playing cards"; and Mr. Warner has here
proved himself a most expert whist-player,
with the fullest understanding of American
leads. "A man always talks badly who has
nothing to say," Voltaire remarked; but it
does not follow that the reverse is true, and
that the man who has something to say is
sure to talk well. Mr. Warner and Mr. Warner's companions in 'Their Pilgrimage' have
always something to say, and something to
which the reader is delighted to listen; and
they say it in such fashion as to make conversation seem the very cream of culture.

In 'Their Pilgrimage' Mr. Warner showed
that he had a firm grasp of the essential facts
of American life and character; in 'A Little
Journey in the World' he revealed that he had
also mastered the art of fiction, and was able
to fix the reader's attention not on the scenery
and the chorus which had amused us in the
earlier book, but on the characters of the men
and women, and on the influence of these
characters one on the other. He had turned
from the externals of existence to the internals.
He had thrust the panorama into the background and concentrated his attention on the
figures in the foreground. And these figures
are well worthy of his attention and of ours.

He groups together the delicate, sensitive New England girl of high ideals and the rather common but clever New York girl—of a kind seen in the city often enough, and yet not at all a typical New York girl, if such an entity may be said to exist. He shows us a new variety of the English lord whom it is the duty of the American girl to reject ; and he makes us see what a fine fellow the Englishman is, and what a mistake the girl makes in accepting, instead of his, the love of a Wall Street speculator, handsome, bold, scheming, and unscrupulous. And here it is that Mr. Warner proves at once his insight into life and his newly acquired skill as a story-teller ; he makes us see and understand, and even accept as inevitable, the slow process of deterioration which follows on the mating of a young woman of lofty standards with a dominating character of coarser and tougher substance. The disintegration of Margaret's moral fibre under the repeated shocks of worldliness, incessantly recurring, until at last the strain breaks down all resistance, seems to me one of the finest things in recent American literature.

At the end of 'A Little Journey in the World,' the gentle Margaret, after wedding the daring speculator Henderson, had suffered a slow moral disintegration, under which she finally faded away and died, whereupon the swift vengeance of Heaven pursued Henderson, and the book closes with his marriage to the easy-going Carmen. That these two characters, thus fitly disposed of in 'A Little Journey in the World,' should reappear in the 'Golden House' is a surprise, not to say a shock, and yet it must be confessed that the result justifies Mr. Warner's daring. We can see now that the author was right in thinking that the career of Henderson, and also the career of his second wife, might be carried further with advantage. Henderson's career, indeed, the author has seen fit to carry out to the end—to his sudden and lonely death in the midst of his millions.

Of all the many attempts to represent in fiction the American money-maker, the man who has amassed an immense fortune, and who goes on increasing it with no thought of resting from his labor, the man who exists solely for the sake of making money, surrendering all tastes that interfere with this passion, giving up everything else, abandoning his whole life to gain, and not from any sordid avarice, not even from any great desire to use what he accumulates, but moved mainly by an interest in the sport of speculation, and finding the zest of his life in the game of money-making, wholly regardless of the cash value of the stakes—of all the many efforts to put such a man before us in the pages of a novel, this study of Mr. Warner's seems to me to be the most successful. Henderson is vigorously presented, and we get to know him, and to understand how it is that he is not unkindly, and that he is absolutely unscrupulous. We perceive why he has no malice towards those he injured by his scheming, and why he bears them no ill will even after he has ruined them. We see how all the better impulses of the man have been starved and choked by the growth of the one all-absorbing passion; and it is not without pity that we discover that not only his impulses, but his tastes, his minor interests in life, his faculty of enjoyment, have been eliminated, one by one, until at last he has nothing left but the one thing on which he has set his heart, and to which he has bent his whole being. Then at length even this one thing loses its savor, and is as dust and ashes in his mouth. At the very acme and climax of his triumph Henderson knows that his life has been a failure.

This boldly projected figure of Henderson dominates the book as his exemplars tower

aloft over the social organization of our time.
In our modern society the millionaire has in
great measure taken the place held aforetime
by the nobleman ; and it may very well be that
we allow him to enjoy too many of the feudal
advantages of his predecessor. Perhaps Mr.
Kidd is right in thinking that we are according
to captains of industry an undue proportion of
the powers and of the honors which were for-
merly bestowed rightly enough on command-
ers in war. One of the merits of the 'Golden
House' is that it forces the reader to take
thought about society. The book is no tract,
no parable, no allegory, no *Tendenz-Roman* even,
as the Germans phrase it, no novel with a purpose ; it is a story, pure and simple, with strong-
ly drawn characters, in whose sayings and doings we are interested for their own sakes ; but
none the less even the casual reader who turns
its pages carelessly has forced upon him a consciousness that our social system is strangely
inadequate and startlingly imperfect.

Perhaps nothing is more harmful to-day than
the frequent denunciations of the existing order
of things with the obvious inference that a society so deformed needs to be rooted up and
cleared away and made over. What ought to
be clear to us is that, with all the defects of

the social organization in our time, this organization is less defective than it ever was before; that there has been steady progress in the world from generation to generation; that there has been no century in which the average man has not been better off than he was in the previous century; that it is our duty to do all that in us lies to help forward this progress; and that nothing tends to retard this improvement more than violent and inflammatory declamation. The pessimist who refuses to believe in any advance is quite as wrong as the optimist who denies that there is any necessity for a forward movement. Now, as always, discontent is a duty, for it is a condition precedent to progress. It is not discontent that throws the dynamite bomb; it is despair.

While Mr. Warner's novel is the work of a thinker, and while it affords food for thought even to the cursory reader, it is wholly free from denunciation. By its perusal we are led not to wish to destroy society, but rather to desire its reorganization; and we are made at least to suspect the complexity of the problem. Mr. Warner shows us the poor as well as the rich—Mulberry Bend after Madison Avenue— and he does not idealize the one more than the other.   Perhaps, after all, the pinch of poverty does not squeeze the soul more than the weight of riches—although it numbs the body sooner.

It is poverty that saves Jack Delancy, who is perhaps to be called the hero of the 'Golden House,' and who is certainly a most skilful piece of portraiture.   We all know Jack; he is the clever young fellow, moving easily through life along the line of least resistance, and having no shadows in his path except when he stands in his own light.   If such a young man has had the good fortune to be born poor, he can save himself, and the world is the richer by a fine fellow.   If he has the bad luck of Jack Delancy, and inherits twenty thousand dollars a year, he is not likely to save himself, for *ennui* is the devil's advocate—and as Mr. Warner tersely puts it, " wherever the devil is, there is always a quorum present for business." Even after Jack marries an ideal wife his fate is in doubt, and it needs not only her aid but the sharp douche of sudden poverty to stimulate him into making the best of his life.

As it is no fairy tale that Mr. Warner is writing, he does not let Jack reform in the twinkling of an eye, but only after a long struggle with himself and his habits; for while a noble impulse may make a man volunteer for a for-

lorn hope, only a firm will can keep him stead-
fast under fire.   It would be futile to wonder
how a Parisian novelist would have treated the
relations of Jack and Carmen, but it may be
doubted whether that treatment would be as
calmly truthful as Mr. Warner's.   The American author knew his type when he made Henderson conscious that Carmen was as " passion-
less as a diamond."

How true to life Carmen may be, and how
accurate Edith Delancy, I do not know; for
how is a mere man to decide on the niceties of
feminine character?   Every novel really worth
criticising needs two critics—a man to discuss
the male characters, and a woman to discuss
the female.   It is easy enough for any man to
say that the heroes of many women's novels
are impossible, for the most part either prigs
or brutes; but may not the woman retort on
us, and declare the irresistible heroines of men's
novels equally impossible?   To us men Carmen
is coherent and convincing; Edith Delancy is
almost flawless, and quite too good for that
very human creature Jack; Dr. Ruth Leigh is
most sympathetically drawn; but what do the
women think of these creatures of a masculine
brain?   I can bear testimony to the dignity
and the strength with which Father Damon is

delineated; but I lack the knowledge to take the stand in behalf of Dr. Ruth, who seems to me quite as well conceived, and quite as happily presented.

In this his third work of fiction the author is more the master of the art than in the earlier studies. He possesses his materials now; he is not possessed by them. He keeps his story more firmly in hand; the construction is solider; the movement is swifter; and there are fewer digressions from the main path. To a certain extent the modern novel is the result of a marriage of the essay and the drama; and it is natural enough that the child should resemble now one of the parents and now the other. In Mr. Warner's hands, as was to be expected, the tendency is rather towards the essay, yet there is no obtrusion of the narrator's personality, and there is no lack of dramatic force in certain of the situations. In more than one of them—in the parting of the doctor and the priest, for example—there is the swift simplicity of tragedy, inevitable, inexorable, final.

(1894.)

DURING the many recent attempts to separate the study of literature from the study
of linguistics, and to consider literature itself
artistically rather than scientifically, an increasing attention has been paid to American literature and to the British literature of the nineteenth century. Here in these two subjects is
matter which the students can readily assimi-
late, and in the treatment of which it is possible for the professor often to excite in them
the first germs of that " taste for reading " that
only too many of our college graduates are
wholly without. For the instructor who wishes
to arouse young men to some understanding
of the underlying principles of literature, a
course in modern fiction may be made even
more stimulant than the two courses already
mentioned. The evolution of the narrative
art, from the 'Gesta Romanorum' down to the
writings of Mr. Howells and Mr. Kipling, its
modification by the practitioners who follow-

ed the Rabelaisian tradition on the one hand and the Cervantine on the other, its increasing complexity, as the puppets *in vacuo* of Boccaccio were followed after many years by the full-blooded characters of Turgenef seen against a background of real life—all these things can be made interesting to the student, who soon finds himself reading the ordinary fiction of the day with some appreciation of its merits and with some understanding of the school to which it belongs.

Unfortunately there is no single book which serves not necessarily as a text - book — in a course of this sort, when the pupils read the authors for themselves, a text-book is almost an impertinence—there is no book to serve as a work of reference even. Dunlop's ' History of Fiction' is hopelessly out of date, even in the late revised edition; and the most of the books about the novel err in considering it only in a single language. Now, if anything is clear in the history of fiction, it is that there has been incessant international borrowing; the principles and the practice of a Spanish author influencing an author in France, who, in turn, may have modified the native manner of an author in England. Mr. Henry James studied his art under Turgenef, and M. Paul

15

Bourget obviously modelled his earlier novels on those of Mr. Henry James. Again, Mr. Rudyard Kipling was a disciple of Mr. Bret Harte, who was a follower of Dickens, who avowedly copied the methods of Smollett, who confessed his imitation of Le Sage, who borrowed the form of the Spanish picaresque tales, which, in turn, may or may not have been derived, in some measure, from the Greek romances.

M. Paul Morillot's 'Roman en France' is a discussion of the novel in France, and Mr. Walter Raleigh's 'English Novel' is a discussion of the novel in Great Britain, while Mr. William Edward Simonds, in his 'Introduction to the Study of English Fiction,' devoting himself chiefly to the English novel, rashly wanders off now and again into a consideration of the great writers of other languages. Of the three books Mr. Simonds's is the least satisfactory. He has no firm grasp on the principles of fiction; he does not seem to be able to follow the steps of its steady progress; he is lacking in the sense of proportion, or he would not be so absurdly inadequate in his treatment of Hawthorne, who is actually introduced and dismissed in the same paragraph with Bulwer Lytton. Mr.

Simonds fails altogether to understand the position of contemporary American fiction. Nowhere does he record the extraordinary skill with which almost every locality in the United States has been translated into literature. Nowhere does he praise the vigor with which American character has been presented by the best of our later writers of fiction. His attitude is often colonial in its deference to the opinion of British critics; and it is through the spectacles of British critics that Mr. Simonds sees not only the American novelists, but the French as well. The whole chapter on the 'Tendencies of To-day' is ill-digested and inadequate; sometimes it is even misleading. One sentence (in which Mr. Simonds declares that "it is not only a perfected art that puts Alphonse Daudet far above Ohnet, De Maupassant, Zola, and the other realists, great and small") is even more startling than the late Walter Pater's setting up of Octave Feuillet as a rival of Gustave Flaubert; it is almost as astonishing as Jeffrey's casual lumping together of Victor Hugo, Balzac, and Paul de Kock as the three great French novelists of his time.

Mr. Simonds fills more than half of his volume with selected passages, specimens of nar-

ration from 'Beowulf' to 'Tristram Shandy.'
M. Morillot also gives up a great many of his
pages to selections, more carefully made than
Mr. Simonds's, and far ampler and more representative than those in the American book.
But I doubt the advantage of a volume of
selections from fiction. Specimen bricks cannot even suggest elaborate structure. Condensation is possible and often advisable; but
mere excerpting is of doubtful utility. Sometimes, as the late Henry Morley declared, the
half is greater than the whole; and probably
it is better that the student should read the
'Decameron' and 'Gargantua' in the compact
volumes of the Universal Library than in
complete editions. Extracts draw attention
rather to the mere writing of the novelist,
to his style chiefly; and they are of little or
no help to us in any endeavor to grasp the
primary conception of a novel, to disengage
the skeleton of the story, to see how skilfully
it is articulated, and to decide for ourselves
whether or not the work has the supreme
grace of form. So rare is real symmetry of
construction in British fiction that Mr. Simonds, for example, cannot understand why
Mr. Henry James should find the Joyeuse
episodes of the 'Nabab' excrescences.

M. Morillot's selections seem to be well made, and the brief notices with which he introduces them are intelligent and to the point. Especially to be commended is his cordiality to Mme. de Lafayette, whose 'Princess of Clèves' was as far in advance of its time as was the best of Miss Austen's equally feminine and equally introspective fictions. His treatment of Alexandre Dumas will not satisfy the neo - romanticists, who hail the author of the 'Three Musketeers' as one of the great masters of fiction; but it is quite in accord with the consensus of critical opinion in France to-day. His assertion that the moral significance of Octave Feuillet's novels is "very virile and very pure" is probably also in agreement with contemporary judgment in France; but it will seem unfounded to many of us who believe nearly all of Feuillet's hectic tales of fashionable life to be profoundly false, and, therefore, to be radically immoral.

Perhaps Mr. Raleigh's is the best of these three books. The favorable impression it makes on the interested reader is due partly, it may be, to the fact that it contains no extracts to interrupt the current of the author's criticism. Mr. Raleigh considers first the origins of the English novel; and then he discusses at length the Elizabethan romances, devoting himself chiefly, I am sorry to say, to their style, and not giving sufficient attention to the underlying stories themselves, almost overwhelmed out of sight by the overflow of rhetoric. (Nowhere, so far as I know, has the actual art of narration among the Elizabethans been adequately considered except in an essay by Mr. R. A. Ashworth in a number of the *Sewanee Review* for 1894.) Mr. Raleigh, while confining himself to the development of the novel in England, follows carefully its expansion in France, and is ready always to point out the influences exerted across the Channel. He also shows what a service was rendered to the art of fiction by the improvement of the art of character-drawing consequent on the starting of the *Tatler*, the *Spectator*, and their imitators. He conducts the history of English fiction only to the advent of Scott; and it is to be hoped that he will be encouraged to carry it forward at least to the death of Thackeray.

Excellent as Mr. Raleigh's book is, with its criticism at once solid and brilliant; with its subordination of mere biographical and bibliographical detail to the more important work of tracing the development of the art itself; with its many merits, not the least of which is its readableness; excellent as it is altogether, it still leaves room for a book about the modern novel which should not confine itself to a single language, but which should show, by a judicious selection of the salient stories of all the nations of Europe, where the novel of to-day got its complexity. The time has come for a history of modern fiction in which shall be set forth the successive steps of the story-tellers who narrated at the first things quite Impossible; and then things only Improbable—in which stage the romanticists still linger even in this last decade of the nineteenth century, when riper artists have already tried to pass from the description of the merely Probable to a depicting of the absolutely Inevitable. The historian of fiction will need self-control if he wishes to declare with precision the merits and the demerits of the masterpieces in each of these four classes.

Neither the future historian of fiction nor the present instructor who is trying to trace the manifold developments of the art of story-telling as it is to-day, will be greatly helped by a very curious little book recently edited by Mr. Richard G. Moulton—'Four Years of Novel Reading: an account of an experiment in popularizing the study of fiction.' It appears that in a group of mining villages in Northumberland near the German Ocean the so-called University Extension movement led to the formation of a society for the study of classical fiction, one novel being read every two months by every member, after an expert had drawn up a list of points to which the attention of readers was specially to be directed. Upon one or more of these points papers were written, and upon others a debate was held. Obviously a scheme like this, well carried out, would do much to enliven village circles, and might even aid in increasing the readers' understanding of human nature. But the experts who choose the books and who draw up the lists of points to be considered, debated, and written about must needs be men of unusual equipment and insight, or else we shall see the blind leading the blind.

The list of the twenty-five novels read by these Northumberland villagers does not inspire confidence in the wisdom of their experts. The object of the course was avowedly to read classical novels—and it included one tale by Mr. Robert Buchanan! The other twenty-four novels were four of them by Dickens, three by Scott, two by Thackeray, by George Eliot, by Charles Kingsley, and by Charles Reade, and one each by Mr. George Meredith, Mr. R. D. Blackmore, Mrs. Gaskell, Miss Brontë, Miss Austen, Dr. Holmes, Victor Hugo, Dumas, and Eugène Sue — surely as odd a selection of "classical novels" as could be made. They are most inexpert experts who are capable of including Mr. Robert Buchanan and Charles Reade and Eugene Sue in a list of authors of "classical novels" while excluding Cooper and Hawthorne, Balzac and George Sand, Turgenef and Tolstoï. And some of the comments are quite worthy of the selections. The editor calls 'Monte Cristo' "a masterpiece of the French school" and "a consummate piece of literary workmanship from beginning to end." Mr. W. E. Norris (himself a novelist) tells us that to have discovered something about the methods by which Tito in 'Romola' "has been made to stand on his feet is, no doubt, to have discovered something about the technical side of light literature":—it is indeed a discovery to find that any man able to read and write is capable of classifying as "light literature" the acute and subtle study of the processes of Tito's steady moral disintegration under recurring temptation.

Although other British novelists—Mr. Justin McCarthy, Mr. J. H. Shorthouse, Mr. S. J.

Weyman—are also among the experts, scarcely once is attention called to the merits of the story as a story, or to the principles of the art of narrative. So slight is the sense of form among British writers of fiction that no notice is taken of the bifurcation of the plot of 'Vanity Fair,' or of the sprawling end of 'Monte Cristo,' or of the beautiful simplicity of structure of 'Silas Marner'—a simplicity not to be seen in any other of George Eliot's novels. In the suggestions of the experts, as in the introduction of the editor, stress is laid chiefly on moral questions, on ethics rather than on esthetics.

(1895.)

THE END

HARPER'S AMERICAN ESSAYISTS

OTHER TIMES AND OTHER SEASONS. By LAURENCE HUTTON.

A LITTLE ENGLISH GALLERY. By LOUISE IMOGEN GUINEY.

LITERARY AND SOCIAL SILHOUETTES. By HJALMAR HJORTH BOYESEN.

STUDIES OF THE STAGE. By BRANDER MATTHEWS.

AMERICANISMS AND BRITICISMS, with Other Essays on Other Isms. By BRANDER MATTHEWS.

AS WE GO. By CHARLES DUDLEY WARNER. With Illustrations.

AS WE WERE SAYING. By CHARLES DUDLEY WARNER. With Illustrations.

FROM THE EASY CHAIR. By GEORGE WILLIAM CURTIS.

FROM THE EASY CHAIR. *Second Series.* By GEORGE WILLIAM CURTIS.

FROM THE EASY CHAIR. *Third Series.* By GEORGE WILLIAM CURTIS.

CRITICISM AND FICTION. By WILLIAM DEAN HOWELLS.

FROM THE BOOKS OF LAURENCE HUTTON.

CONCERNING ALL OF US. By THOMAS WENTWORTH HIGGINSON.

THE WORK OF JOHN RUSKIN. By CHARLES WALDSTEIN.

PICTURE AND TEXT. By HENRY JAMES. With Illustrations.

16mo, Cloth, $1 00 each. Complete Sets, in White and Gold, $1 25 a Volume.

PUBLISHED BY HARPER & BROTHERS, NEW YORK.

☞ *The above works are for sale by all booksellers, or will be mailed by the publishers, postage prepaid, on receipt of the price.*

THE ODD NUMBER SERIES

16mo, Cloth, Ornamental

PUBLISHED BY HARPER & BROTHERS, NEW YORK.

☞ *The above works are for sale by all booksellers, or will be mailed by the publishers, postage prepaid, on receipt of the price.*